Federal Aid to Private Schools

Federal Aid
to Private Schools

by Leo R. Ward, C.S.C.

NP

The Newman Press • Westminster, Maryland
1964

Imprimi potest: Howard J. Kenna, C.S.C.
Provincial Superior

Nihil obstat: Raymond F. Cour, C.S.C.
Censor librorum

Imprimatur: Leo A. Pursley
Bishop of Forth Wayne—South Bend
Febraury 29, 1964

Contents

v

Federal Aid to Private Schools

1 · A Closed Issue?

It is remarkable and really incredible how rapidly the climate of opinion has been changing in regard to any possible federal aid to parochial and other private schools. Leaders of distinction, in the fields of politics, education and law, some of whom had been silent and some of whom had been opposed to it, have now spoken in favor of aid. The same must be said of journals: some that had opposed it have yielded ground, whereas others that had been silent have begun to raise the question. Conferences of religious leaders have been held; for instance, at the University of Chicago in 1962 and 1963, and in New York City in 1963. Church groups have proposed and some have actually held open inter-faith discussions of the issues, and a Gallup poll has indicated a notable swing in public opinion.

The somewhat perplexing case of Senator Abraham Ribicoff may illustrate how vital the question is to the public. As long as Mr. Ribicoff was a member of the federal Cabinet, he went along literally with the Administration's reiterated claim that "across the board" aid to church-related schools would be unconstitutional. Unfortunately, "across the board" is not a legal or constitutional term, and, in the contexts of its use by Secretary Ribicoff and the late President Kennedy, the press and the populace took it to mean that, although some aid to church-related colleges would be constitutional, no aid at all to church-related schools would be allowable.

But as candidate for the Senate from Connecticut, Mr. Ribicoff disavowed the position attributed to him and said that his own personal view was that some types of aid, even on the lower levels, would be constitutional; and as Senator he has proposed and vigorously defended not only aid but a detailed six-point program of how it might conceivably be given.

On entering office, President Kennedy took what all understood to be a strong stand against aid to church-related schools on the lower levels, and his doing so could be understood in the light of politics and especially in the light of his having repeatedly declared for that position during his campaign. Once elected, it would have been strange and next to impossible for him to crawfish. We may, however, make three suggestions: first, that he did not anticipate the vehemence of the opposition his views were actually to encounter; secondly, that, with his prohibition of "across the board" aid, he did not absolutely close the door; and, lastly, that he would have been happy if presented with a compromise formula, as indeed one of the men closest to him hinted. In a talk at Columbia University in 1963, President Kennedy's advisor, Theodore Sorensen, said these words: "While it should not be impossible to find an equitable constitutional formula to settle the church-school aid problem, it is difficult for the formula to be suggested by the nation's first Catholic President."

Educators of national stature also have been declaring

for at least a reconsideration of the question. Robert M. Hutchins, always frank and direct, allowed little space for nonsense. Here is what he said at the University of Chicago conference in 1962: "I am for Federal aid to parochial schools. I am for Federal aid to anybody who will do a sound educational job." Our leading national educational statesman, Mr. Hutchins added that "the wall" has no future because "it cannot help us learn." Professor Francis W. Rogers of Harvard University has declared: "An inequity exists when the citizen must forfeit the benefit of his tax money solely because he exercises his freedom of choice in his selection of a school for his child." To date, the most notable of the statements by educators, we would say, is that by William Brickman, professor of the history of education at New York University, who said three things: first, that if "separation" is taken to mean absolute separation, "there never was a Church-State separation in the United States, especially in education"; secondly, "separation" should be as applicable to loans as to grants, and to religious schools as well as to religious colleges; and, lastly, that the Jewish community, to which Dr. Brickman belongs, has been "one-sidedly devoted to a dubious doctrine of separationism."

Some Protestant leaders and groups have also shown a willingness to discuss positions, with a view to at least an understanding; and Reverend Dean M. Kelley, who is an official of the National Council of Protestant Churches, has said that as long as Protestants continue to accept aid for their own institutions, they may scarcely complain when others ask for comparable aid. At the same time, we must of course recognize that most Protestants are adamant on the problem and that for a long time to come most of them will remain so. Yet the statements of leaders and groups, combined with a popular poll, suggests a possibility of considering the issues.

With much consistency, Jews have been against aid to religious schools. However, this stand is by no means universal and monolithic today, as indicated by the remarkable declarations of many prominent Jewish leaders—Ribicoff, Brickman and Lippmann—as well as of Jewish groups, the influential *Jewish Forum* having said (May-June 1962) that it "reverses its 44-year old position of opposing Federal aid to parochial schools"—a reversal which no doubt shocked many Jews.

Other journals that were either mum or "anti" on the central issue when, in 1961, President Kennedy first spoke to Congress on education now favor some aid. The Chicago *American* stated in 1962 that it favors aid to parochial schools because they provide "so important a share of the community's total educational facilities" and that the problem "should be studied carefully and calmly." *Christianity and Crisis* devoted an issue of May 1963 to a reconsideration of the problem of aid, and again in October it followed up with an editorial, signed by such leaders as Reinhold Niebuhr, John C. Bennett, and Robert McAfee Brown, urging "experimentation, openness to new ideas, willingness to reason and discuss."

Most interesting of all has been how *The New Republic* has reversed its stand; and, since its present position is so much one with that taken in this book, we shall outline what the editors now say. In the issue of March 20, 1961, they were rigidly and exclusively for aid to public schools, mainly, they said, because of those schools' "nationalizing and equalitarian work," and against aid to private schools, because, it was believed, to accept the principle of support for private and public schools equally would be to give up what the editors took to be the mission of the State in education: "It is committed to exerting a secular, unifying, equalitarian force." However, an editorial entitled "Church-Related Schools" in the issue of March 2, 1963, declared for some aid, publicly supervised, for church-related schools, and said: "A more serviceable approach is that the State should legislate for purely secular ends, but that it should not worry if this incidentally helps a church." Since the State's concern is that all should have a grasp of certain subjects, it may, the editorial continued, subsidize the pursuit of them, and need not ask whether Jesuits or Lutherans give the required instruction. If a "strict constructionist"—an absolute separationist—should object that, at least in the hands of Jesuits or Lutherans, there is no strictly secular subject and every subject has religious significance, the editors granted there is truth in the assertion, but appended this note: "Interpretation and belief are intrinsic to any instruction."

Added to the declarations of political and educational figures, of church leaders and groups, and distinguished journals, are the yet more decisive statements by legal and constitutional experts, men from the finest law schools in the nation. These we merely mention at present, as we shall have occasion to cover their testimony in context.

While these many challenging changes were taking place, the House and Senate of Michigan (the twenty-first state to do so) were passing a law allowing bus service to all school children, and Governor Romney, signing the bill, said that less than this service would be unjust. The Governor of Iowa, himself a Methodist, in his first message to his Congress (1963) proposed such service. Intermittently, too, political leaders, educators, and economists have made out a variety of plans by which they say aid could constitutionally be extended, in some form and measure, to every child or to his parents.

It is true that in opposition to the witness from the types of areas we have indicated, one could readily find powerful countering statements from just those types, with the exception—we must affirm—of the legal and constitutional experts. For instance, as recently as May 1963 the St. Louis *Post-Dispatch*, usually a liberal journal, wrote: "Public funds for buses are the same as public funds for schools." Add to that assertion the following report of the 1963 declaration of several church groups: "Spokesmen for the National Council of Churches, United Presbyterian Church in the U.S.A., and Baptist Joint Committee on Public Affairs told Congress they remained firmly opposed to federal aid for Church-related elementary and secondary schools."

Granting the existence of entrenched positions, we nevertheless see no reason to mitigate our claim that the tide of better-informed opinion at this time is running to the side of reconsidering the possibility and advisability of some aid for private schools.

To the surprise of everybody, popular opinion likewise has evidenced a sudden movement in the same direction. Of course, we must not make too much of a popular poll, but we may simply remark that the Gallup poll showed an incredible shift of opinion from March 1961 to February 1963. The pollsters' issue was federal aid to "Catholic and other private schools." At the earlier date, Protestant voters were 63% against this aid, but early in 1963 the figure had come down to 50%.

No one knows all the factors that have gone into the change of either popular or informed opinion. Among potent influences have been John XXIII, a Catholic president, and citizens' organizations, notably the inter-faith Citizens for Educational Freedom (3109 South Grand Blvd., St. Louis, Mo.), who, in the year ending October 1963, doubled their membership, distributed a million pieces of literature urging parents' rights and freedom in education, provided popular support for free textbooks for all Rhode Island children, and at least helped to obtain bus service in Michigan. But it may also be that many people, parents and citizens as well as experts, are more maturely reconsidering the question, and are wondering what "the wall" is doing to freedom of choice in education, to education itself and to the national good, if this "wall" is kept "impregnable"—as a man on the Supreme Bench said it always should be. In any event, reconsidering aid and "the wall" is the order of the day. To conclude this matter for the present, let us notice the reconsidering that has been done by Walter Lippmann. In his column of March 14, 1961, Mr. Lippmann was, to put it mildly, unfriendly to aid and he then literally took the absolute view expressed by Justice Black in the *Everson* case of 1947—the view that no tax money may be used for religious purposes; and at that time Mr. Lippmann thereby ruled out aid to church-related schools. Two years later, Mr. Lippmann had considerably altered his view. In a televised program on May 1, 1963, he said: "It is not beyond the wit of man, if he means it, for us to find a way of aiding education, whether it's in public schools or parochial schools, without getting involved in the question of teaching religion. . . . We have five million . . . to be educated in these parochial schools. They are part of the American system of education. . . . If they're going to be educated in them, they should be educated as well as possible; therefore, if they need money, as private schools do, for textbooks, or laboratories, or even buildings, I think a way should be found of getting rid of this religious knot that we've tied ourselves into."

What all the cited statesmen, educators, religious leaders and journalists are saying is what the legal experts had been saying for years—at least since the *McCollum* decision (1948). The fact is that there are many cracks and holes and leaks in "the wall." Not that these leaders force a crack or leak, but merely that they point out that the wall has always had cracks and leaks in it. Why did intelligent citizens not know this all the time?

The answer has to be a bit roundabout. Anyone studying the present subject is confronted by and must be impressed by three obstacles not only to any possible aid but to so much as frank and open discussion of any aid to students in church-related schools. One obstacle is the longstanding myth built up around the words *separation* and *wall*, a myth that has been read into Supreme Court decisions. Another obstacle is the renewed and consistently heavy emphasis placed on "separation" as absolute since two of the Supreme Court decisions, *Everson* and *McCollum*. This explains how it was readily possible and as if routine for President Kennedy, speaking of conceivable aid to religious schools on the lower levels, to say, "There isn't any room for debate." Thus our ordinary free way to proceed, through discussion and debate, was to be forever closed. The third obstacle is an animus against church-related schools, an animus which one can sometimes notice in some Protestant spokesmen and journals and very often in declarations made by national educational associations, and which one must think arises in part from fear of the unknown.

Each of the obstacles is considerable, and since they aid

and abet each other and their strength multiplies geometrically, it takes much care and circumspection to keep the relevant questions open and to get scholars, not to say citizens, to review and study them. When therefore we say in this book that the proof of a particular matter is easy and simple, we mean that it really is so—"really," that is, from the point of view of history, expert opinion, current events and logic; but we must also admit that from the point of view of psychology and the mass mind, the same point may be extremely difficult to prove. For instance, it is easy and simple to show that in our country, Church and State have always collaborated and do now collaborate; but given the three obstacles multiplied geometrically, to make this point convincing is far from easy and simple.

No doubt we do argue in this book, though it should be enough to state, that absolute separation is a condition which we have never had in practice from Washington's day to ours, and would not want in theory. But a deeply felt myth says we have absolute separation, and a myth is a formidable psychological hurdle. Then, too, almost all of us have recently been attempting to build up a lesser myth to the effect that there is a constitutional difference between a high school student and a college student, so that the latter but not the former is eligible for loans or grants; and we have been attempting to create a twin minor myth to the effect that all must attend a monolithic type of school in order to be thoroughly American. Some men of distinction—for example, Robert Weaver, Nathan Pusey, and James B. Conant—are victims of this minor myth of the thoroughly American school. Major or minor, the myths are blocks to freedom of thought and action.

Those three obstacles make the task of Americans, whatever their color or faith, all the harder if they wish to begin to give frank and open consideration and debate to the issues involved in aid or no aid to religious schools. The three, we repeat, are the myth expressed in the words *separation* and *wall*, the deepening of the separation-and-wall idea by various words and decisions of the Supreme Court (has not the Court said that "the wall" must be kept "high and impregnable" and did not Justice Frankfurter use the words "absolute separation"?) and, thirdly and far from least, an animus against private and church-related schools.

Take just one illustration of the triple hurdle. At the first national session (1962) of the National Conference of Christians and Jews Religious Freedom and Public Affairs Project, a lawyer for the Civil Liberties Union said, in perhaps intemperate language, that it would not do "to break asunder the wall" of "a complete and absolute separation." Here we see how even professed believers in liberty can club the public with the "wall" idea and with the myth of absolutes. We see also why a thing which in itself may be easy to prove may in concrete circumstances turn out to be difficult.

Actually, the argument of this book is simple. It is in part that the private and church-related school, strictly an indigenous American institution, has been and is now state-aided; that there has been and continues to be among us much collaboration between Church and State, and again among Church, State and all kinds of schools; that a single monolithic educational system would not only be unfortunate but un-American; that to pressure private and church-related schools into mediocrity would not only be unfortunate but would be a denial at once of religious liberty and of freedom of choice in education, a freedom declared in the *Pierce* or *Oregon* case of 1925; and that the total educational enterprise of the United States can and ought to find ways of turning itself into a unified and pluralistic national effort to educate all children, as President Kennedy urged, to the peak of their ability.

We are therefore going to insist that an over-all pluralism in education is sure to demand more of us—as private and as public educators, and as citizens—than we have conceived up to now at all generally. Private and public education rarely work together for the common educational good. This they must learn to do.

For the sake of simplification, this book stands aside from the debate whether the nation's schools need federal aid. But if the taxpayer's money is to be given to some schools—and it is now given generously—it ought, in some form and in some amount, to be given to all schools.

Why to all if to any? Because American citizens must seek the maximum development of every youth's capacity. Every youth should have this development, and if, as is the case, some parents use their guaranteed freedom of choice in education to send their children to religious schools, then those children should not be penalized for their parents' use of that guaranteed freedom of choice. Parents and children would find a price tag placed on freedom.

Private schools, religious or other, should either be disallowed, and all schools be required by law to become state schools, or law and practice should make it reasonably possible for private and religious schools to enable their students to achieve maximum development. Here we at once encounter a basic dilemma. We cannot bless crippled and ineffective schools, and we may not disallow citizens' freedom to patronize private and church-related schools. It would seem that something will have to give, either freedom on the one hand, or on the other the quality of church-related schools and the good of the child and the nation. The dilemma must stand if separation and an educational Berlin wall are absolutes.

We believe, however, that something better can be done than the destruction either of freedom or of the quality of education and the good of the child and the nation. At least the issues of freedom in education, on the one hand, and, on the other, of quality and the child's and the nation's good must be kept open. In the changing climate of opinion, and with the issues openly debated as they are today, we may hope that the education of children will be advanced, along with the enlightenment and freedom of the nation.

2 · Native American

The Wider Framework

To speak of "separation" and the schools, we have first to see this problem, itself complicated, within the wider and more complicated set of national problems and purposes in education. The reason for viewing our problem within the wider framework is that it belongs there, and it is time that those who argue that "separation" does—or does not—allow government aid to private schools should take a comprehensive and full view of American education.

On the education issue, every American has to be "pro" one thing above all, and that is the real education of all American children regardless of creed or color or social status. This attitude of standing for the education of all is a requirement of nature as well as of democracy.

The second reason for taking a fuller view from the outset is that for a long time most of us proceeded as if we had quite simple educational problems, if any at all. Today everyone can see that for too long we had all been complacent and content with easy answers. The man who then rated as the top educational professional in the author's state of Indiana boasted to assembled teachers a few years ago that, having visited France, he knew ours was a better educational system than that of the French, because we kept our children in school many more years than did the French, because proportionally as well as absolutely we had more children in school, and because he had seen some French children cry when they were officially declared unadapted to the higher learning.

That has been one of our main assumptions: bigness is a virtue in education: the bigger the numbers in school and the longer they are in school, the better. The earthquake that brought us to our educational senses was Sputnik. We had been debating scarcely a fundamental relevant thing, so sure were we of ourselves. Now and then, there had been a ripple on important though secondary issues; for example, whether all should have the chance to go to college, whether there were enough classrooms, how the schools and colleges could accommodate the big influx of children in the post-war years, whether a non-communist Marxist should be allowed to teach in a public university, whether oaths should be required of teachers, and whether congressional committees were too severe or perhaps too lenient on academic and scientific freedom.

The quality of education for every child must always remain the radical issue; and that means above all the quality of basic education. We may therefore say thanks to Sputnik for making us reconsider. Educators have been coming round, and we may hope they will more and more come round to see and to act. At this stage of our national life and thinking and especially of our national attitudes on so radical and pervasive a problem, this is as yet only a hope. Why should anyone say this? Take straws in the wind. Even today some of us are still going around in the same old circles of a frontier quantitative pragmatism. Many suppose that the educational system, now spending billions, would, if given another billion or two, automatically be all that anybody could desire. It is assumed that if federal money were given to public or private primary and secondary schools, someone would appear to spend the money wisely, and the schools would be better. A national education officer has said that, the twelve years from kindergarten through high school having (he conceded) proved inadequate, the answer would be to add two years to that long period. It is as easy and mechanical as that—the bigger the better, the longer the better. More money and more years would certainly do it.

All admit that more time and money could be a real assistance. We raise this neglected side of the vast national problem only to suggest that some are still going around in the mechanical treadmill and making the same easy and complacent assumptions. Think of the billions now spent. Think of the man-years and woman-years on the part of teachers and students now spent on education. The moral is that we must be further and more generally shaken out of our national educational lethargy. In the meantime, we need a less naïve standard of excellence than "the bigger the better."

Besides the hurdle of such a false premise, we will have the task of shaking ourselves out of the *status quo*, and this is always difficult to do.

Fortunately, the most vital portions of President Kennedy's messages to Congress on education—and these were not the tax and money portions—stated in broad outline what must be done, and at what point it is most important to work. In his 1961 message on education, the President called for "the maximum development of every young American's capacity." Of course, it is permissible to take President Kennedy's words either as a platitude or as political talk. Yet we think it better to receive them in their literal good sense and to make a national concerted effort to carry out the proffered formula. His words were too good and vital and far too relevant to be brushed off. They were simple and straightforward and said exactly what should be said. Their inclusiveness also was right; no half-way measure, no compromise, no discrimination. "The maximum development of every young American's capacity"—this stated the over-all national problem. Educators must work to find out what it means to go with that formula, not merely or mainly because it came from a high political source, but because it stated a truth which nature itself enjoins on parents and teachers and all who are concerned with education.

Education is the bringing up of the child, and in a democracy it is the bringing up of every child. A stunted upbringing will not do: the demand of nature and the times is for maximum development. Nor will it do to develop some and neglect others.

On record is the statement of what we must consider the generalized and continuous national problem in education. The problem is twofold; it is the problem of quality in education and the problem of universality of quality in education: "maximum development" of every youth. It is easy to imagine, too, what this principle, if carried out, could do in a single generation to reduce juvenile aimlessness and delinquency, to mention merely one issue.

The second statement by President Kennedy defined where we must begin. In his 1962 message on education, he said we must begin with basic education. Take these relevant words: "Elementary and secondary schools are the foundation of our educational system. There is little value in our efforts to broaden and improve our higher education, or increase our supply of such skills as science and engineering, without a greater effort for excellence at this basic level of education."

This principle, too, is obvious and must be accepted in theory and practice. Given our present situation, the point is also urgent, and we wonder that so little has been made of it. In sum, it was as if the President was giving us in the two principles a simple and yet invaluable blueprint for education.

Fortunately, competent critical studies of the national educational situation have been coming from the press. In 1963, citizens and educators were the beneficiaries of two extraordinary studies of American teacher education. Based on much close and painstaking research, James D. Koerner's *The Miseducation of American Teachers* was a disturbing revelation, and it has been followed by James B. Conant's *The Education of American Teachers*, which, also based on firsthand inspection, contains a long and useful list of steps that need to be taken. Some years ago, Abraham Flexner reported that the condition of medical education in America was far from satisfactory; and his candid and extremely critical report did great good. So too we may hope for results from these 1963 reports on the education of teachers.

Studies appearing in 1961 made it clear that our elementary education is defective. We refer in particular to *Tomorrow's Illiterates*, edited by Charles Walcutt, and to *What Ivan Knows That Johnny Doesn't* by Arthur S. Trace. Whether these studies are on all points the scientific last word is waived. Take them with a fifty per cent discount, and their effect remains devastating, the former reporting that a completely illiterate boy graduated, with an A in English, from a public high school in the state of New York. If we are the least bit serious about either education or freedom, the impact of the reports made in these books will be like that of a new Sputnik. Dr. Conant's *Slums and Suburbs,* also 1961, is likewise far from a flattering report of our educational achievement.

A few primary schools, among them a distinguished one in Washington, D.C., called the Amidon School, have demonstrated three important facts about basic education: first, that the young child's education is frightfully deficient in reading and numbers, the subjects most vital to his future development; second, that children can do far better work than they are doing; and third, that they like to do it. Hence, when in this book we speak about the propriety and even the priority of the education of man's spirit and about freedom in education, we are aware that the basic education of beginners in reading and numbers, now so deficient, is absolutely fundamental and is incomparably *the* educational problem. A few years ago, some of the professionals in education took the propaganda of the Basic Education people to be the work of poorly informed men. No sensible and informed person considers it such today.

Happily President Kennedy said in effect that there was no use turning the pyramid upside down and trying to make it stand on its apex. We must see to quality in the education of children, and Carl F. Hansen's *The Amidon Elementary School* (1962) shows that this can be done.

The over-all national problem, within which our problem must fit, is therefore clear. It is the development of every child's total capacity, and this, as Kennedy so well said in his 1962 message, demands that we start with the basic education of little children. Every child now spends years and years in school. If we are not getting top-quality results, there is something wrong: perhaps with attitudes, perhaps with assumptions, perhaps with practices and methods, perhaps with philosophies. In spite of all our controversies over federal aid for universities and for research, it is conceivable—nobody seems to raise the question—that we have been starting at the wrong end.

We have repeated and enlarged on the two most important statements on education by President Kennedy for the good reason that they go far to sum up what must be aimed at in the national situation and in every school, and also because Kennedy went directly to the point: he declared for the good of the child and the nation, and not for the good of the school, as the end. It is true and unfortunate that he himself never felt quite free to go through with the basic principles so well outlined by him, but held back somewhat and compromised, and seemed after all to mean that provision should be made for only part of the nation's children. Yet we think that, because his own program kept failing to get off the ground, President Kennedy for one would have been willing to allow time and discussion the chance to work toward some more viable program.

We proceed then on several assumptions, among them that open discussion of the issues is demanded, that basic fairness is wanted by all, that the present practice of "allowing" private and church-related schools and yet in effect denying them the means to be strong and effective cannot last, and that freedom in education will, given our people's love of freedom and justice, be worked out with due respect for "separation" and in the climate of an accepted "pluralism."

The Radical Problem

In this chapter, our problem at bottom is the problem of freedom of choice in education. It naturally falls within the body of problems outlined by those two wise statements coming from President Kennedy. Our problem is "separation" or the "separation principle" and government aid to children and youths in private educational institutions. Does "separation" of Church and State allow or preclude aid to children in private schools, even if those schools are church-related? The First Amendment to the Constitution (Art. 1 of the Bill of Rights) reads: "Congress shall make no law respecting an establishment of religion, or prohibiting the free exercise thereof." Would it necessarily be contrary to this Amendment if state or federal tax moneys were in some measure at some time used to enable parents to choose—as is done, for instance, in Holland—church-related schools on the primary or the secondary level? Again, suppose such moneys were used to furnish the advantage of much-needed good teacher-training for the children attending church-related schools, or good lighting or good playgrounds for the children—would the spending be always and necessarily unconstitutional? This is a fair and somewhat difficult question, at times asked or answered with considerable emotion and acerbity. (Incidentally, neither the word *separation* nor the word *wall* is in the Constitution. "Wall of separation" is a figure of speech used in a letter by Jefferson when he was president.)

Our position is that some governmental financial aid may constitutionally be given either to parents making the choice, or to children attending private schools of all types and on all levels. At least, the question of its possibly being constitutional and within the best American practice to furnish some funds for some of the educational purposes of those children and their parents must be kept open. To close the question in an absolutistic fashion would be high-handed and arbitrary.

It is seen then that we—along with many others—disagree with the absolute position of Justice Black in the 1947 *Everson* decision and the 1948 *McCollum* decision. The gentlest description of Justice Black's statements in those famous cases is that he was therein a strict con structionist, and we think it fair to designate his position as the absolute or the never-never position. Part of what he said was that neither the state nor federal government "can pass laws which aid one religion, aid all religions, or prefer one religion over another."

Justice Black's first and second negative statements we take to be wrong, and the third quite in line with American experience. The State may aid—and in our country, for better or for worse, the State perpetually has aided and does aid—religion and religions. Of course, the State may not pick and choose and prefer.

Anyone holding with Justice Black's dictum would appear to be on somewhat doubtful ground, and this we shall proceed to show. Stated as a double negative, our own position is that the never-never and the never-can doctrine is an unfortunate error, and precisely because it turns the relative into an absolute and attempts to negate too much. Before we go on to see wherein the dictum is erroneous, we mention in passing our agreement with the central point decided in *Everson*: that the State may pay bus fares of children going to parochial schools; and we do not disagree with the central point decided in *McCollum*: that the State should disallow the use of public properties and public-school time and systems for the ends of sectarian instruction. Our disagreement is only with Justice Black's dictum, or aside, in each of the cases; and in spite of his warning, it is difficult to take the quoted statements as anything but an aside and not at all as the main point decided in either of the cases.

Part of a National Whole

Our thesis is that aid in some form and in some measure is allowable. The first step in proof is one of the easier and simpler steps we shall be obliged to take. It is to indicate that private schools, church-related ones included, are a *part of our entire national educational establishment.* This they are in two important senses. First, they are a part now; traditionally and historically they have always been a part, and we cannot find a time when they were not at least a part. It is another thing to argue that they should not be a part or should never have been a part; in any event, they have been and are a part. We are merely stating an historical and a current fact. There they are and there they have been, and to discuss education in America or to make financial or other policies for it as if they did not exist—as is often done—is like proceeding on the supposition that New York, which is and always has been a part of the Union, did not exist. How the citizens of New York State would like that, and how unworkable the supposition would be.

But not only are the private and church-related schools an historical and an actual part of the national whole. They are, secondly, a legally and officially recognized part of it.

Proof that they are is open to everyone's inspection. One proof is that the State requires, and for the national good it undoubtedly should require, that private schools, including the church-related, meet certain legal stipulations; for example, in regard to teacher qualifications, the number of days taught, the subjects that must be taught, and the safety of school buildings. A second proof is that the student credits for most types of private schools are officially recognized—"accepted" is the word—and students may transfer from private schools to state schools without question. It is quite a different matter when students wish to transfer from schools in India or Brazil to American state schools, and it is different because in America there is no legal and official recognition of Indian or Brazilian schools. And how could there be? Our private schools are a legal and official part of our schools, whereas Indian or Brazilian schools are not. That is the basis of the difference. A third proof lies in the fact that a private school may sue in United States courts. A private military academy and some private schools operated by nuns carried the Oregon public-schools-only law to the Supreme Court of the United States and that Court, recognizing their right to do so—their "standing," as lawyers say—abrogated in 1925 the Oregon law which otherwise would have destroyed them.

Thus in everyday practice, the law of the land says several significant things to church-related and all private schools: "You must meet such and such standard requirements, your students may freely transfer to state schools, you may sue in court, and the Oregon decision publicly declares your constitutional right to exist." All this is to say that the State legally and officially recognizes private schools, of any kind and on any level, as part of the national school establishment. Because of these legal sanctions, they are a *de jure* part of that establishment, just as because of their historical and actual existence they are a *de facto* part of it.

An immediate consequence is that an action by the State which would, directly or indirectly, tend to nullify the right of private schools to exist and effectively operate would be contrary to freedom and justice. A preferential distribution of school-tax money could have this effect. A second consequence is that parents have the right by the Constitution as well as by nature to educate their children, and that the declarations by Clayton Hutchins, an official of the Department of Health, Education and Welfare, are false and exceedingly mischievous. Mr. Hutchins said that parents have "no inalienable and constitutional rights to regulate the education of their children. There is only the privilege granted by the state." If Mr. Hutchins meant to speak for the totalitarian state, his statements were correct.

Serving a Public Purpose

Teamed with that first step in our proof is another which is just as much an open book, just as readily comprehensible, and also just as vital and important as the first step. *Schools serve a public purpose.* This is true of any and all kinds of justified schools, public and private, church-related or other, technical and liberal schools, universities and kindergartens. This public-purpose feature of schools, obvious though it is, must be emphasized. Of course, schools are good for those attending them, and they may be good for the homes affected by them, and for churches that may in various ways be among the beneficiaries of schools—of state schools, church-related schools and other private schools. But in the present context that is not the whole point, nor precisely the point of prime interest to the State. The immediate point is that schools serve a public purpose and serve the general welfare. They must do this, and "must" in two senses. First, it goes with the nature of a school to serve a public good and, secondly, all of us would be up in arms against any school or any professor teaching anything inimical and derogatory to the general welfare and the good of society. This goes without saying in any society, and it is the reason why we refuse to let known communists teach in private or public schools; they are committed to teaching communism as the way, the truth and the life, whereas we hold that such teaching is not only false, but is sure to be detrimental to the public good.

This point about schools serving a public good is so obvious that, although it should certainly be emphasized, it is outside reasonable argument. Courts naturally take it for granted; it is important to them, but evident. Schools are to serve the child and the public—that in brief summary is what any and all defensible schools are for. Some schools are private, some public. At least we may speak of private and public schools in the ordinary and popularly received sense of "private" and "public": in the minimal sense that the so-called "public" are the object of more tax benefits than the so-called "private." (We shall see that each type is favored by tax benefits.) But it would be unrealistic to say that Harvard University, a "private" school, serves no public purpose, and that only state universities do so. It would be just as unrealistic and meaningless to say that a Lutheran grade school serves no public purpose. If it serves none, it should be closed. In the author's neighborhood, in recent years, an excellent private school has been established for little children capable of superior work. If this school serves no public purpose, it cannot be justified.

Take out the word *school* and put in the word *hospital*, and the same principles are readily seen to apply. The large hospital in Chicago known as Cook County Hospital serves a public purpose. And so of course do private hospitals, including the church-related ones, such as Mercy Hospital and Presbyterian General Hospital. Because all such Church-related hospitals are non-profit corporations *and because they serve a public purpose*, tax benefits—city, state, and federal—are accorded to them as well as to other types of hospitals, and federal grants made to them, no line of demarcation or discrimination being drawn against any of these public-service institutions. The reason is quite simple: public service merits public recognition; and hospitals, whatever their religious or non-religious affiliation, serve a public purpose.

What we have said about schools and hospitals must be said also in regard to other beneficent institutions—homes for crippled and retarded children and for the feebleminded, and rehabilitation centers for alcoholics and victims of dope addiction, some of which institutions are operated by the various faiths. All these institutions serve a valid public purpose, and it has become the custom of the state and federal governments to assist them financially, not only with tax preferments but with loans and grants, to enable them to fulfill this public purpose. Part of the logic at the bottom of this encouragement and immense public aid to private and church-related institutions is that the State, if it is helping public-purpose institutions, should draw no line of demarcation or discrimination against a public-service unit merely because it is operated by a religious body; and such was the decision of the Supreme Court in the famous *Brad-field* case, mentioned below.

Some citizens and groups, fighting strenuously against financial aid or relief for church-related schools, go along happily with such aid and relief to church-related hospitals—an interesting fact to which we shall return. As far as hospitals are concerned, the famous legal decision defending the right of a private hospital, church owned and operated, to receive money from the federal government was that rendered in the District of Columbia's *Bradfield* case in 1899, and this has become what lawyers call a "leading case"; that is, others are patterned on it. The District had been working hand in glove with a private church-related hospital and paying money to the hospital for services and accommodations. The decision rendered by the Supreme Court said that the fact that the individuals composing the private, church-related corporation belonged to this or that religion was "not of the slightest consequence with reference to its incorporation," and the persons furnishing the services could not, on the grounds of their religious belief, be qualified or disqualified to do the work or to receive pay for it. The relevant fact was that the operators of the hospital, whatever their belief or disbelief, were performing a service that the government needed and wanted performed. In 1962, the federal Supreme Court refused to consider a similar case; a Kentucky hospital, built and owned by the public, was being operated by nuns who were paid for their work. The 1899 decision had already settled this Kentucky case. The United States does not require a profession of faith from those doing a public work.

In all the types featured—schools, hospitals, reformatories, and the like—it is easy to see the reason for spending tax money as in fact we do. We spend it not to help some favored son, not to assist the private venture of an individual or a corporation (for instance, to aid and abet the Lutheran or Jewish or Catholic church), but to help a corporation or institution freely to perform a public service and do a public good. In furnishing tax money to such bodies, legislators have to take into account only whether the money furnished out of taxes is being spent for a public purpose. Is a needed public purpose being served or not? That is the decisive question. Whether the private corporation or institution is or is not a religious body of Jews or Christians or secularists must be disregarded, as the Court said in the District of Columbia case. The essential point is that public money is being spent to do a public work.

At the same time, the money may indeed serve the good of a religious body, of Jews or Christians or secularists, and thus serve a dual purpose. It serves a public purpose at which the State first of all aims, and also a private and religious purpose at which, according to the separation principle, the State may not directly aim. The State may neither exclude nor directly seek the religious purpose.

The relevant principle was stated in a quiet but effective way by Justice Frankfurter in his concurrence in *Mc-Gowan* v. *Maryland* (1961). He said that American law and the Constitution merely require the implementing of "other substantial interests than the promotion of belief." His words were a brief statement of the dual-purpose principle. Remembering that the Justice had, concurring in the *Everson* case (1947), declared for what he called "absolute separation," we must think that his statement of principle in 1961 was tantamount to a rescinding of that absolute position and a return to consonance with constitutional history and common practice. We shall have occasion to refer again to his 1961 statement, which certainly should excite interest since it looked so much like a crack in "the wall."

"Other substantial interests than the promotion of belief"—in one way or another, this principle is often reiterated by the Supreme Court. Justice Clark quite clearly appealed to it in the Bible and Lord's Prayer case of 1963. In considering any legislative enactment, the test questions, he said, should regard its purpose and its primary effect. If either of these is either to advance or to inhibit religion, the enactment is constitutionally unallowable. "That is to say that to withstand the strictures of the establishment clause there must be a secular legislative purpose and a primary effect that neither advances nor inhibits religion."

These were the decisive phrases: "secular legislative purpose" and "primary effect," and these two phrases, when combined, say what Justice Frankfurter had said in the words "other substantial interests."

Of course, a private institution such as a hospital, a church or a school may, as a private person may, refuse to accept government aid. That would be its choice and its business. Some religious groups, notably some Lutherans, have said that if government money were offered to their schools, they would refuse it. They would be entitled and perfectly free to do so; the State would presumably not pressure anyone to receive it; nevertheless these same Lutherans gladly avail themselves of government aid to their hospitals and churches. More consistent was a religious group which did refuse government aid in a remarkable instance. During the depression of the 1930's, public money was used to build schoolhouses for Amish communities in Pennsylvania. This was meant to be a dual-purpose action which was aimed primarily at a public good, though many may have thought it would at the same time help the sectarian group. The Amish would have nothing to do with those buildings. They might or might not; the government was willing, in its own view, to go out of its way to help the Amish while it concurrently served a public good. But to refuse the offer was within the option and choice of the group.

The money is furnished by the State to a private hospital or other private institution, and its purpose is to help individuals and the public good. The acts of legislators are always serving dual purposes, and even multiple purposes. This is common and everyday, and there is nothing recondite or revolutionary about it. For instance, the state builds a highway. This serves many private interests—business, schools, churches, recreation. No doubt it serves the State in some of its directly official business, but most of its service to the public good is through serving an ensemble of private goods. In that way, it serves "the public" and "the body politic"; and if roads were precluded from serving private and religious purposes, we would have few "public highways" built. If legislators were to shy away from all action that might serve private interests concurrently with serving a public good, they would never be able to do anything at all.

The idea of dual and multiple purpose should be familiar to every citizen as well as to legislators. The word one chooses to employ, "public good" or "public purpose," is the matter of least importance. As a substitute for such a word, we might speak of the "public service" they perform. Or we might say that they serve the common good, as they obviously do. Some persons speaking responsibly use still other words, such as "the national purposes" or "the national interest," and they speak of "dual-purpose legislation" and "dual-purpose institutions."

A Functional Idea

Whichever word is used, it is easy to grasp this uncomplicated idea, which could be assimilated by the average high school student. But it is a significant functional idea, and this for three good reasons. First, it is in part on this ground of public service that aid is given in any form, such as tax relief, and in any amount, to churches and synagogues, or to church-related schools and hospitals or any other private schools and hospitals. It is most properly on this ground of public service that aid may be claimed. Hence our insistence in these pages on the public-service idea. In any instance, aid is claimed and given for value received, and not as a friendly gesture. Second, because of public service rendered, it may certainly be argued that help should be given (waiving, just now, whether it really is given or ever was given). Third, it is always going to remain difficult to draw the line in helping church-related institutions—the line between helping the public good and helping, almost with intent to help, the sectarian institution—and again to draw the line between how much or how little help (if any at all) should be given in view of the public service rendered. It is hard to say just where to cease giving, because more giving might amount to directly helping a church or other private institution in its private and sectarian capacity.

It is easy to see how to draw the line in each of the two cases mentioned, that of *Bradfield* in 1899, and again in the Court's refusing to review the Kentucky case brought to its attention in 1962. In the latter, nuns were employed by the public to operate a hospital and, of course, were paid to operate it. But the public—city and state—owned the hospital. Some persons and groups said the practice should be stopped, because, they maintained, the practice violated the "separation" principle. How was it thought to do this? Because the nuns and their religion presumably were in some way helped, and this helping of the nuns and their religion was affirmed to be against the First Amendment's provision that Congress shall make no law concerning an establishment of religion. Now, it may well be that the practice was in fact helping the nuns and their religion. But that is not what was aimed at by city and state. These wanted a good public work done, the nuns were the people available to do it, and it would be discriminatory and unreasonable and contrary to the free exercise of religion to begin scrutinizing the faith of persons employed by city or state or nation to run a hospital, to build a bridge, or to win a war.

Nevertheless, it is at times difficult to draw the line between, on the one hand, seeing that a good and needed public work is done and, on the other, preferentially aiding a particular religion. In other words, if church-related schools are aided—and all are now, in various ways, aided—it is sure to be difficult in many instances and at many points to distinguish between the sacred aspects of their work and the public-service aspects. That was a difficulty picked up with fine sensitivity by Justice Jackson in the most famous school-and-church case yet decided by the Supreme Court. In the *McCollum* case, various religions had been teaching their tenets in a public school, and the delicate point raised by Justice Jackson was that it is impossible to see precisely where the secular leaves off and the sacred begins. Take the instance of New York City working, as no doubt it well may, with the medical arm of the Jewish Yeshiva University. This is a dual-purpose working in which the city goes about its business and aims at a public good, though incidentally and of course knowingly the taxpayers' money which is spent is also an aid to a sectarian religious group, namely a Jewish body. The city's duty is to work for the public good, and this it may do by working with a private religious group which, in serving the public good, also serves a religion. That is what is meant by "dual purpose."

Oddly enough, too, since the *McCollum* decision, the Court itself has added, if that could be done, to the difficulty—or perhaps we should say that the Court has discovered that the difficulty is almost as great as Justice Jackson had then said. The Court has said, in what the profession calls a dictum or an off-the-cuff remark, that humanism or ethical culture or even secularism itself is a religion. If the Court is to say that some action is tantamount to an establishment of religion, it must have a working idea of "establishment" and of "religion." But aside from this "secular sectarian" issue, drawing that line between secular and sacred must always be a delicate prudential process, and neither in regard to hospitals or schools nor in regard to churches and synagogues will it ever be easy and simple to keep the line clear and distinct.

Happily for the State, that fine line of distinction, just how far to go and where to stop, is not what the State has primarily to consider. City or State has first of all and most of all to consider the public good. This it has to do, and this is all it has to do. Whether the achieving of the public good is done through a school or a hospital, and whether it is done through a city school or hospital or through a private one, church-related or synagogue-related—all this is secondary to what the city or the state is as if by oath bound to do.

3 · Collaboration

State Helping Church in America

So much, then, for the private school in the two basic respects so far featured—*a*) as an American institution both historically and legally, and historically a more venerable institution than the White House; and *b*) as serving a public purpose.

Next we take up a third point, and this in itself (though not always in the public mind) can be kept as straightforward and intelligible as the preceding ones. Some may think it in fact an obvious point, but we are bound to elaborate it. This we must do, not merely for the record, but because, being so patent everywhere around us, it might be overlooked; and the American public today needs the shock effect of this fact as fact.

The new point is that church-related and other private schools have always received state and federal aid of a financial kind, they continue to receive it, and are almost certain to continue receiving it. As a proper prelude to this point, we are going to cite in the present chapter many well-known instances of the State's aiding religion in various ways, financial and other, in the United States, and then in the next chapter deal with the fact of the State's helping private schools. Our thesis is therefore dual: that there is and always has been collaboration of many and various kinds between State and Church in the United States; and this will be followed by the thesis that there is and always has been collaboration between private schools, including church-related ones, and the State. It must be emphasized that there has been, there is, and presumably will be much collaboration. Is this to be considered an evil circumstance? That is a question not plainly within the purview of this book. We are referring to what is and has been and presumably will be, and not to its possible good or evil.

If our thesis proves to be correct, then the famous dictum of Justice Black in the *Everson* bus case (1947) will be seen to be false, and, in choosing to lean on the Black dictum, President Kennedy will be seen to have chosen an ultimately dubious support. Part of what Justice Black then said was that neither a state nor the federal government "can" pass laws "which aid one religion, aid all religions . . . no tax in large or small can be levied to support any religious activities or institutions . . . the clause [in the First Amendment] against establishment was intended to erect a wall."

Justice Black's absolutist statements have been controverted by legal and constitutional experts (for example, Professor Corwin of Princeton, Professor Sutherland of Harvard, and Professor Kauper of Michigan), the refutation being the fact that our government now aids religion and has always done so, and that when State and Church— as is the case—work together in many enterprises, it is at best ambiguous to say there is a "wall" between them. Nevertheless, the absolutism of Justice Black and others must continue to be refuted, and not just once, but again and again. This is so because many persons have become confused and really believe that such assertions as Justice Black's represent the historical and actual situation, and because we may be sure that some, not believing such assertions at all, might at times use them in a Machiavellian way to advance and defend political and religious interests. And for a third and far more important reason: Justice Black's assertions in the *Everson* dictum, although out of line with American history and practice, rest on a venerable myth, the myth of "the wall," and it takes long-range working and much patience and repetition to make a dent in a mythical wall. Scholars such as Dr. Kauper of Michigan Law School and Dr. Sutherland of Harvard Law School, who are experts and professionals on legal and constitutional history, have refused to accept Justice Black's absolutism generally, and particularly of course in *Everson* and *McCollum*. But the experts are only a small part of the total population, and they are not the myth-makers.

Now for the proof of our present thesis: that the State in fact aids, and often even financially aids, the Church in the United States, and has always done so. (Whether it aids too much or too little, and whether at times it has aided unwisely, are likewise debatable points.) For convenience, it will be preferable to number various types of aid to the Church, with no intent to list them in the order of importance.

First. A most interesting case of federal aid to religion is seen in the financial aid which was given for generations by the federal government to missionaries among the Indians. This aid was originated in the presidency of

George Washington, was approved by him, and continued unbroken for over a hundred years. As early as 1789, Congress allocated funds for the support of Christian missionaries working among Indians, an action later recommended by Henry Knox, our first Secretary of War, and approved by President Washington. According to the literal statement in American State Papers, the purpose was not only dual but multiple: "The object of this establishment would be the happiness of Indians, teaching them the great duties of religion and morality, and to inculcate a friendship and attachment to the United States." That overt multiple purpose is worth repeating; the purposes were the Indians' happiness, their life of religion and moral duty, and friendship to the United States (purposes in part akin to those of twentieth-century overseas spending). Literally included was the teaching of morality and religion. This may have been an oversight, or it may have been political heresy; at any rate, it was included. No doubt incidentally though really, the propagation of the missionaries' faith was also an effected end, along with what Justice Frankfurter in 1961 so well called "other substantial interests." As everyone is aware, the "no establishment" clause, if taken literally and absolutely, would at once rule out as unconstitutional the aid to missionaries blessed by Washington in an early day and by others for more than a century.

Challenging, however, is the fact that precisely this kind of aid was approved also by President Jefferson himself, who, two years after he wrote his famous letter about the "wall of separation" between Church and State, disregarded the same "wall" by asking the Senate to ratify a treaty with the Kaskaski Indians, a quite innocent thing (one might suppose) to request. But was it so innocent, and was not President Jefferson disrespecting the "wall"? Innocent or guilty, that is what he did, and in somewhat surprising circumstances. A Catholic priest was just then teaching those Indians, baptizing them and building a church, and the remarkable thing was that a federal allowance of one hundred dollars a year was made to him for his work and an outlay of three hundred dollars to build a church. On Jefferson's recommendation, the Senate went through with this "no aid to religion," and President Jefferson not only went through with it, but even led the way. (The well-known Jewish lawyer, Leo Pfeffer, who often opposes the "religion in education" cases before the Supreme Court, was asked on a 1961 television program what he made of the financial help immemorially given to missionaries among Indians. He replied that the money was given to the Indians.)

Financial aid to Protestant and Catholic missionaries among Indians is only one of many instances within this exceedingly expansive type of aid to religion. It is not only Indian missions that have been the beneficiaries; for example, government checks with President Taft's signature on them went to Christian missionaries in the Philippines. Any one instance—and there are scores of them—would be enough to cast doubt on Justice Black's universal and absolute negative.

Second. It is the custom to furnish chaplains for both the federal Congress and for the congresses of some states. This practice, which presumably aids the State, is obvious aid to religion, and it is unlikely that any of those chaplains, most of them Protestant, have ever regarded it in any other light. The chaplains are paid out of tax money, federal and state, to do a religious work and, we must think, primarily a religious work. Supporting religion in this way is much more than financial support, since it is official political recognition and encouragement of religion. The author is neither approving nor disapproving the practice, but merely saying that it is among the facts of American life. Whatever else it is, the practice means that the federal government—and on occasion this or that state government—goes through with the dual-purpose idea, one of the achieved purposes being effected by the giving of both financial and moral aid to religion. (The *McCollum* decision said in 1948 that for representatives of religious faiths to enter public schools in order to teach religion as requested by parents of school children was unconstitutional because it meant using tax-supported property and state-commandeered time to propagate religion. One wonders what properties those inveterate congressional chaplains may sometimes use.)

Third. Strictly out of public funds, chapels are built and maintained on government property for the military. This is something we Americans do in many lands, at home and abroad. Also out of public funds all sorts of equipment is supplied the chaplains of any and all faiths; for example, furniture, Bibles, altars, chalices, wine, candles, medals, rosaries, and church-related schools. The military go much further and on occasion actually pay, out of tax money, to have their children educated in church-related schools, conducted by military chaplains or others. During World War II, for instance, some church-related schools in Newfoundland, where United States troops were quartered, were paid fifteen dollars per month per Armed Forces' child. The head of one of those Christian schools has said that the American tax money thus received was a help in more senses than one.

It is easy to say, as if in rebuttal, that men and women

in the Armed Forces are away from home, and some of them conscripted. This is true, yet in fact no one was conscripted into the service until April 1863, and most military personnel in America have not been conscripted. In all such instances and no matter whether the forces are or are not conscripted, it is beyond doubt that government and government money are helping the churches. That is not what the government sets out to do, but that is what it does. The State is helping the Church, and the Church is helping the State; this is not "separation," which few would desire in the situation, but a collaboration which the vast majority have always desired. This collaboration kills two birds with one stone; it helps the nation and it helps the churches. We might say that the chaplains do even better. They serve their churches, serve the military personnel, and serve the nation. If anyone prefers to defend this inter-working and collaboration of the State and a faith—whether Jewish, Catholic or Protestant—as "separation" of Church and State, we refuse to argue about this somewhat special use of words.

Fourth. With federal tax moneys, chapels and chaplains are maintained at West Point and Annapolis, and attendance at chapel services is compulsory—a practice which might appear contrary to the *McCollum* decision. This procedure is another instance of the State's aiding religion, now this religion, now that, and in fact, whatever about intention, aiding all religions; and this we suppose is done without a shadow of discrimination. As in the other instances, so in this: there is evident financial aid to particular religions and to all religion, and also real and effective moral and psychological assistance given to each and all. No amount of casuistry can hide so plain a fact. What is happening here, also, is the collaboration of Church and

State, and the good work done simultaneously for Church *and* State—plainly a dual purpose work—is done by the Church and paid for by the State.

Fifth. We mention in particular that to help the religions—Jewish, Catholic and Protestant—a school was built and maintained in Germany after World War II for the purpose of training teachers of religion for the three faiths. Uncle Sam paid the bills. Also one may refer to "Character Guidance Discussion Topics" which were published by the United States Army (in Europe) in three series in 1957, and in which we read such phrases as "one nation under God" and "dependent upon—responsible to—Almighty God." Uncle Sam was footing the bill, undoubtedly in order to help the Armed Forces, though at the same time he was helping religion and the religions. It is easy for the Armed Forces to surmount the insurmountable wall.

Sixth. Chaplains are fed, clothed, housed and serviced at penal institutions, another evident instance of the State's helping the Church in order to help itself. This is common practice, and certain chaplains at Sing Sing have made national reputations for serving the public good, in the service of which they are invaluable and precisely because they are serving their Hebrew or Christian churches. As in the preceding examples, the chaplains are serving both the Church and the State—quite a showcase illustration of Church-State collaboration for a dual purpose. In this as in all the examples already mentioned, the churches serve a public purpose and at least in effect work for the common good, so that not only does the State help the Church, but the Church reciprocates by helping the State.

The two servings—to Church and to State—are simultaneous. Churches work for the good of the State, but they work also for the good of the churches. Precisely as churchmen, that is what the chaplains are there for—namely, to promote a religious work. Only a man with his tongue in his cheek would dispute this. Yet at the same time the State wants the churchmen there to help the State. Strictly parallel to this dual purpose service—to religion and nation —is the dual purpose service performed by the many chaplains in state and federal hospitals and in old soldiers' homes.

Seventh. People give thanks to God. That is their business and their churches' business; so at least we may suppose. The churches ask people to give thanks to God, and the request is properly within the orbit of their functions. Annually now for over one hundred years, the President also asks the American people to give thanks to God. Is it really his business to go urging and exhorting in religious matters? Is he not going considerably out of his way? Is the President justified in turning preacher? Cobbler, stick to your last! "We give Thee thanks, O Almighty God, for all the benefits we have received from Thy bounty." This looks like either a private act or a public work to be done by believers and their churches. Why do the State and the President busy themselves with it? So at any rate the political absolutist as well as the belligerent secularist, communist or non-communist, might well ask. But whatever the absolutist and the secularist may say, it has been American practice for over a century for the State and the President to collaborate with the churches and urge citizens to give thanks to God.

The most recent Presidents have done what their predecessors have always done—promoted the collaboration of Church and State. In his first broadcast to the nation, President Truman asked all the people to pray to God for him. Among many collaborative acts, President Eisenhower made public declarations for and with the churches during

Religious Emphasis Week, and President Kennedy asked citizens to dedicate an annual day to asking God that all men might have a full measure of dignity, freedom and brotherhood, and he himself met at a Prayer Breakfast with Congressmen who had the custom of blessing the day with the Lord's Prayer. President Lyndon Johnson concluded his first speech to Congress with these words: "And on this Thanksgiving eve, as we gather together to ask the Lord's blessing and give Him our thanks, let us unite in those familiar and cherished words:

> America, America,
> God shed His grace on thee,
> And crown thy good
> With brotherhood
> From sea to shining sea."

Whatever a particular president believes or disbelieves, in all such instances as those just cited (and they might be multiplied) he is effectively constrained to work with religion and the churches and synagogues. In effect, the people dare the president to refuse to serve religion. Presidential neutrality toward religion is unacceptable, a hands-off policy is unacceptable. This is seen, for instance, in the way we make our presidents go to church.

The American people would hardly elect a man president unless he somehow seemed to be a man of God, and they would see a man of divorce and easy re-marriage as a dubious candidate for president. Suppose a man is no church-goer at all and has never given public evidence that he is a believer. Even that man, as soon as he wants to be taken seriously for a national office, has to make himself religiously acceptable by going to church or synagogue. If he gave overt contrary evidence, he would certainly be done as a national candidate. Though theoretically the courts could protect him, the people would not; that is how intolerant we the people are in regard to collaboration of Church and State. In a word, we expect a man in high office, whatever his possible personal beliefs or his scepticism, to be an honor to religion and to be working effectively with religion. Americans demand a collaboration—almost a union—of Church and President. Even if religion in a president or in the people themselves were only a façade, our mores would require the president to pay tribute to Justice Douglas' remark, in the *Zorach* released-time case (1952), that we are a religious people—a remark which, by the way, echoed the statement by Justice Brewer, in the *Holy Trinity* case (1892), that "this is a religious nation."

Eighth. "In God we trust" is as venerable an American formula as "One nation under God." People may argue about how much the "In God we trust" formula now actually means even to a believer, let alone to a secularist; but all admit that it *is* on our coins and that it carries on a custom almost as mandatory for us as the custom of having stars and stripes on the Flag.

Subsidizing Freedom to Believe

Ninth. In the area of taxes, we encounter State favoring Church to a remarkable degree, almost as if, in our American way, the State were inexorably committed to do this. Here religion and the churches enjoy many notable aids and preferments, and probably few churchmen or churches and synagogues would be anxious to relinquish their long-standing tax-remission privileges.

In his *Religion in America*, Dr. Willard Sperry, of Har-

vard Divinity School, wrote: "The most important governmental recognition of religion in America is the exemption
of church property from taxation." At times it does happen
that some well-meaning rabbis and Protestant clergymen,
fearing any possible merging of Church and State, say that
church-related schools on the lower levels, most of which
are Catholic, should not receive any state or federal financial assistance, the argument resting on the premise that
any aid to those schools would be a merging of Church
and State and would be contrary to the separation principle. It may be suggested that there is a touch of incon-
sistency in their doing so, since their own as well as others'
churches and synagogues are the beneficiaries of much real
aid, and if their churches and synagogues were to be taxed
tomorrow exactly as are the properties next door, we may
be sure that many of those same rabbis and clergymen
would at once register a serious national complaint. There
is not a synagogue or a church in New York or Chicago
that is pulling its own weight in the matter of taxes. This
means that synagogues and churches of all faiths are gov-
ernment-subsidized.

Churches and synagogues also receive police and fire
protection gratis, in many cities their water supply is free,
and in some areas even the license on their cars has been a
gift of the public. We are not asking whether any or all of
this should be so, but merely remarking that churches and
synagogues do receive much assistance in the form of tax
relief and various gratuities.

Such aid *is* aid, and it means non-separation in historical
and present fact. That is, it means an accepted collaboration
of Church and State in America.

What this tax relief amounts to from a practical point
of view may be variously stated. It naturally comes to a

considerable sum in dollars and cents for each religion, Jewish, Catholic and Protestant. But it also means something in a totally different order. It means that, for good or for ill, religion is state-favored and government-favored in America. *It means subsidizing people's freedom to believe in God and to worship God as the believers and worshippers choose.* It shows that the following editorial assertion in *The Christian Century* (Feb. 1, 1961) was outside American experience and somewhat unreal: "American Protestants will never pay taxes to support Catholic schools." The assertion is unreal since we are all paying taxes to help support each others' religions, and anyone who pays taxes is helping to support Catholic and Protestant churches and all types of synagogues. In practice, that is the American way, whatever of good theory, good constitutionality and fine sentiments. We have found that it shocks priests and preachers and rabbis to be informed that their work is subsidized and that the subsidy means a collaboration of Church and State.

Though the fact of exemption from property taxes is an open book, it may be well to cite three sentences on property tax exemptions from the 1952 edition of *Taxation and the American Economy* by Professor William H. Anderson, of Southern California University: "Institutional exemptions include churches, charitable and benevolent fraternal organizations, literary and scientific societies organized on a nonprofit basis, colleges, universities, and cemeteries. These exemptions are usually from all property taxes except special assessments. The presumption is that the institution in question is performing duties which the state itself is bound to discharge and the general public benefit is greater than the loss in taxes." In other words, the presumption is that churches and synagogues are doing in freedom a good work which the State itself wants done, and this is another way of saying that a dual-purpose is being served.

Of course, churches and synagogues and church publications fall within the classification of non-profit institutions, a circumstance which does not in the least change the fact that they are aided by tax exemption and mailing privileges.

Tax preferments for churches, synagogues and religious establishments are many and various. Gifts are tax-deductible when made to churches, sectarian colleges, and schools of divinity; in this way, the churches gain what the general taxpayers lose. There are tax preferments for establishments that print such matters as religious journals and religious calendars. Besides, in the increase in mailing costs in 1963, one noticed that the mailing of matters religious still left the mailing cost lower than regular mailing costs. The cost of mailing regular magazines is now four cents for the first two ounces, and two cents for each additional ounce, whereas for religious magazines each additional ounce goes at one cent. This is just another in an endless series of ways and means whereby the State helps churches and synagogues and their works. Again, we need take no sides on the propriety of the preferments; for our present purpose, it is enough to refer to the fact.

It is unavailing casuistry to claim that in such instances the State does not give any tax money to religion and the churches. It does give them money, though by indirection and not in hard cash, and this is a point we might as well get clear once for all. If one man pays taxes and another, on similar properties, pays none, the latter is money in the pocket. Likewise, the State ordinarily gives the churches, church publications and church schools no money. It just does not take money from them. In dollars and cents, the net result is the same. Take a parallel case. Today, churches and church-related properties pay insurance to private insurance companies. Suppose that tomorrow, all insurance had to be paid to the government, as all taxes now are, but suppose that the State then said—as it does now in regard to property taxes—that church-related buildings need pay no insurance fees. The State would be giving no money to the churches—it just would not be taking insurance money from them. In dollars and cents, the net result would be the same. The State would be subsidizing the churches, though in a new and additional manner. Or take this parallel. Suppose my friend the grocer never gives me any money, but suppose he never takes any money from me when I buy groceries from him. He is a remarkable help and stand-by, and it would be correct to say that he is subsidizing me. So too of the State when it does not levy all the regular taxes on churches, church properties, church publications and the mailing of them, and on church-related and other schools.

We say these things thus simply and no doubt in a somewhat preachy manner because all ought to know them. Lawyers and judges and justices and clergymen and teachers and journalists ought to know them, and so of course should high school students. These truths express matters of elementary American history and American practice. In regard to tax preferments, the point is that the State is leaning over backwards to aid and assist religion and churches and church-related works. The massive evidence from the area of taxes, if it were taken by itself and in disregard of evidence from the many other areas, makes it clear that Justice Black was speaking unrealistically and somewhat loosely when he said: "Neither a State nor the

Federal Government . . . can pass laws which aid one religion, aid all religions, or prefer one religion over another." The approved practice of both the state and the federal government is to aid religion. We must return to Justice Black on *Everson* in many contexts, and for the present merely repeat that only his concluding words match practice: government may not "prefer one religion over another." Of course, to prefer any one religion would in effect be like setting up a state religion. Justice Black's other words—that government may not pass laws which aid one religion or aid all religions—would have to be taken to refer to something outside American history and customs. Americans pass few laws which aid religion, but many of our well-sanctioned customs and practices, tantamount to laws, are an immense aid to religion and to churches of every faith.

Justice Black's assertions in *Everson* were backed up on that history-making occasion by assertions just as strong by the late Justice Rutledge. Intent on specifying what was the purpose of the First Amendment, Justice Rutledge spoke memorable words in a dissenting opinion. This, he said, was the purpose of the Amendment: "It was to create a complete and permanent separation of the spheres of religious activity and civil authority by comprehensively forbidding every form of public aid or support for religion." He was taken to task by many professionals and experts, since it was as if Justice Rutledge was unacquainted with our tax system and the generous tax preferments historically and actually enjoyed by churches and synagogues, church properties, and church publications, the grants to missionaries and to sectarian schools, and the series of well-sanctioned practices already detailed which have always thrown Church and State so effectively together. What is the propriety of all such "aid and support"? Of that we are not speaking, but again only of the facts.

In some sort of ideal state, perhaps there could be the "complete" and "absolute" separation of Church and State envisaged by Justice Rutledge and others. We have never had that degree of separation, and it may be doubted whether any actual state has ever had it.

Other Preferments

Tenth. As a matter of record, some additional preferments outside the area of taxes should be mentioned. In the United States, in contrast to the custom in many modern and all ancient nations, the clergy and church workers are the beneficiaries of three interesting special privileges. The first is in regard to military service, to which our American clergy are not subject; they may volunteer to enter this, but are never obliged to do so. Theirs is something much more decisive than a deferment; it is outright exemption, and this privilege extends to *bona fide* clerical students. Secondly, closely teamed with this privilege is the fact that, for religious reasons, children, at their own choice and their parents' choice, are free not to salute the Flag when other children salute in a public school. In this regard the *Gobitis* case and the *Barnette* case are famous, and the latter has become what the legal profession calls a leading case. The Gobitis children had refused to salute the Flag in patriotic exercises in a Pennsylvania public school, and the Supreme Court of the United States decided—*Minersville District* v. *Gobitis*, 310 U.S. 586 (1940)—against the freedom of the children and their parents. But in the second or *Barnette* case, three years later, the decision was in favor of freedom, the Court reversing its Gobitis position and declaring that the Flag had been used unfairly as an instrument to impose a religious test as a condition of receiving the benefits of public education. We mention the two cases here because the second decision, reversing the first, was in effect an instance of the State's aiding freedom not only in the abstract but protecting and aiding the freedom of an actual group's worship. In other words, the decision said that the United States was prepared to go a long way to protect and abet religious freedom, and such protection is an obvious aid to religion, the State running to help the Church and allowing primacy of commitment, not to the State itself, but to the Church. What the *Barnette* decision said was, in effect, this: "Let these citizens worship as they freely choose to do—in spite of and in total disregard of a reasonable act reasonably enjoined by the State."

The third particular privilege is concrete too, though today more important in principle than in fact. This privilege allows clergy and church workers to ride at reduced rates on most railroads and many bus lines in the United States and Canada. It is not that the transportation system runs to help the Church. The State does so. The State sees to it that churchmen and church workers have the privilege of traveling at reduced rates.

Consider, then, for a moment two of the particular privileges, that in regard to military service and that in regard to travel. One is a real aid to manpower in the various faiths, the other a real financial aid to churchmen, and each is officially and nationally approved by government.

Consider, too, how the many instances add up—in fact, how they multiply geometrically. They mean that the State has the habit of collaborating with the Church and that it finds a great variety of ways to do so. And more than this, they mean that religious freedom in America has a preferred status even over other highly approved freedoms, such as freedom of speech and of assembly. In our country, the State is perpetually going to great lengths to collaborate with the Church. No matter what anyone may wish or may think is really the case, the three traditional Western faiths, Jewish, Catholic and Protestant, find themselves today in a friendly atmosphere in America; to put it mildly, they are encouraged and are free to develop. The Protestant body long had the hegemony, and, as Professor Littell shows in *From State Church to Pluralism*, some Protestants—whom he considers retrograde—would still cling to that favored position; but today there is, at least on the national level, a general freedom and encouragement for all faiths. We see Church-State collaboration everywhere—in chaplaincies, equipment, missions to Indians, requirements and allowances at West Point and Annapolis, immense and concrete tax preferments, military exemptions, travel privileges, and no requirement to salute the Flag. Each and every one of these aids religion, and all of them are within the standard practice of the Church's being aided by the American State. Taken together, they form the actual and accepted, and seemingly acceptable, American way. Some may choose to say that between Church and State, collaborating so extensively and intensively, there is separation. We cannot understand words so used. There is a distinction between Church and State in our country. That is obvious. But what does this mean? Simply that one cannot be reduced to the other or do duty for the other; each is itself, with its own nature and being and freedoms, its own ends, its own means and methods, and its own work to do. But it should be evident to all that there is remarkably close cooperation between the two, each helping the other with its work, as the types of instances which we have cited make evident. Distinction and endless co-operation-collaboration, and therefore not any literal and absolute separation—that is what stands up like a mountain in both historical and contemporary American fact. It is difficult not to see a mountain, and difficult to dodge one.

For the moment, we close this part of the over-all problem with words from one of the most clearheaded philosophers that America has ever had. In his *Reason and Law*, Morris R. Cohen said: "The failure to discriminate between *distinguishing* and *separation* is one of the great obstacles to the advancement of real understanding."

Hospitals, Yes! Schools, No!

So much for now in regard to direct-line government aid to religion. Some may suggest or argue that the aid is unconstitutional or, if constitutional, that it is overdone or even that in the first place it is bad policy and therefore sure to be bad practice. We keep repeating that the aid is an evident fact, like the wart on a man's nose.

Next, we emphasize the aid given to such institutions as church-related hospitals. To furnish this aid—and it is difficult to find citizens who oppose it—is to aid religion. The aid, part of which is federal and very great, fortunately goes to all kinds of hospitals, public and private, and with no hint or suggestion that some—for example, Jewish or Catholic or Mormon—should be denied the aid. Naturally the aid is given on a public-purpose idea: the hospital is doing a good work which the community should see is done, and the hospital needs help in order to do that work. The assistance is an effective aid to the hospital, whatever the beliefs or disbeliefs of those running the hospital; and in cases of church-related hospitals, we must think that on occasion it is also an effective aid and comfort to the Jewish or Catholic or Protestant religion. Almost all people would at once say: "Good for it! Let's have more of it!" What everyone has to concede is that it is an instance of State and Church working together.

Besides, if the State were to aid only non-religious and state hospitals, which let us presume to be secular, it would, in view of recent Supreme Court decisions, be discriminating in favor of secularism or what has been called secular sectarianism and would thus be "establishing" this secularism as the national religion. We refer, of course, to the words of the Court in *Torcaso* (1961) to the effect that secular humanism is a religion, and even more particularly to the statement by Justice Douglas in *Zorach* (1952) that if the State were to hinder and inhibit freedom for religious instruction, it would "be preferring those who believe in no religion over those who do believe."

If state and federal aid may constitutionally be given to Jewish and Catholic and Protestant homes and schools for the handicapped and to hospitals, one would like to know why aid may not constitutionally be discreetly given also, in some form and some measure, to promote some of of the work done in church-related primary and secondary schools. At least, it seems that one could scarcely with good grace accept and profit by aid in the former instances and argue totally against it in the latter. And what we say is what Reverend Dean M. Kelley, a Methodist minister and himself an official of the National Council of Churches, is quoted as saying to Protestants: "How can you oppose giving to Roman Catholic parochial schools when your colleges and hospitals have been taking Federal money for years? It is apparent that the churches cannot have their cake and eat it too. Either we are going to have to modify our custom of accepting with modest reconciliation what money is offered us, or we shall have to give up our opposition to having money given to other groups."[1]

---

[1] From an Indiana village came this news item in the 1960's: "The vacation Bible school opened Monday, with an attendance of 85, in the high school building. The school will continue for two weeks. Nursery, beginners, primary, junior and intermediate classes are held for any child in the community, regardless of church affiliation."

4 · Aid Given to Private Schools

Preferments and Grants

Our next point is yet more direct since it emphasizes the aid of various types given today, not simply to churches and synagogues and their hospitals and publications, but actually to church-related and other private schools. Some of the types naturally overlap with the aids to religion already summed up; all kinds of tax preferments certainly do. Our procedure will be to list the four main types of aid in fact given to church-related and other private schools.

The first is tax benefits and preferments. In this way, schools of all kinds are subsidized—schools called public and those called private. Schools are thus subsidized whatever their type and whatever their level, from kindergarten through the grades and high school, and through the college and university and every sort of institute for advanced studies. This subsidizing is unquestionably an aid to schools, and in the matter of tax preferments, no discrimination is practiced against church-related or other private schools on any level. Harvard and Yale enjoy this subsidy, and so do Notre Dame and Yeshiva, and so do Wheaton College and Gustavus Adolphus; and just as surely as any of those, so do Catholic and Lutheran and Jewish high schools and primary schools. This way of subsidizing by tax relief is as good as gold deposited in the bank for the school, as all persons and corporations paying taxes well know.

We now repeat and must return later to the fact that this tax subsidy goes to schools in both the higher and the lower brackets. This is the ordinary American way, and at least in recent years only in one state have state-wide attempts been made to revoke this aid for church-related schools. In California, unsuccessful attempts have been made to revoke this status, by referendum or otherwise, and the inference seems to be that there is considerable animus in that commonwealth against private church-related schools on the lower levels. American practice is and has always been on the other side; all types of schools have consistently been free from the general tax load.

One principle encouraging the tax subsidy to church-related schools is non-discrimination, which, of course, is basic to a pluralistic democracy. At the same time, the subsidy given to private schools of all kinds is certainly to be seen also as a defense of freedom to operate such schools. In 1956, the Supreme Court refused—Justices Black and Frankfurter dissenting—to review a California case demanding state tax for properties used for educational purposes; and in 1962, the Supreme Court refused—eight to one, Justice Black alone dissenting—to review a Rhode Island case demanding that the state should tax church property. Which means that, although the Supreme Court has in recent years sometimes been unfriendly to religious practices and teaching in public schools, it continues to leave in peace the age-old tax preferments for churches and church-related schools.

Needless to say, there are many actual and many possible ways in which tax preferments can aid schools, and we merely mention now and will later emphasize that if there were massive tax money spent on public schools only, then private schools of all kinds and on all levels would be at a serious disadvantage, would be sure to suffer, and some would undoubtedly be destroyed. To make it extremely difficult for church-related institutions, educational or other, to exist would be an interference with the free exercise of religion. We shall return to this problem.

2. The second general type of aid to private schools is through grants, the most direct kind of money aid and the most easily understood. Suppose a city grants seven hundred thousand to build a public-school gymnasium or library or science laboratory with all due equipment. The school itself pays nothing, and it has no philanthropic donors; it is given the money out of taxes; or—what amounts to the same thing—the new building is put up and equipped, and, the school standing by, the city or the state foots the bills. Or suppose that a small city allocates five hundred thousand to pay teachers' salaries for the year. Such would be direct grants.

Any grant such as those suggested is a direct and open subsidy to the school, and it is only owing to the grant and subsidy that the public school can exist and operate. What we usually call public schools and state colleges and universities exist and operate on these subsidies, the schools having practically no income of their own, and the colleges and universities having far too little non-grant income. On the contrary, what we call a private school on any level does not in our country ordinarily have these particular subsidies. We say "ordinarily," since neither the state nor the federal government has been in the habit of paying salaries or putting up classroom buildings or gymnasiums or libraries or laboratories for private schools, church-related or other. Even on a matching basis, dollar for dollar, government rarely if ever does so in America, though the question whether state or nation should do so is now seriously debated. Any such building or the paying of any such salary has been uncommon, but today the federal government—no doubt on the public-purpose and dual-purpose idea—has come round to help support church-related colleges and universities and their professors in many interesting projects, though at the same time by-passing grade and high schools.

In some democratic nations, the government does put up part or all of the money to build and maintain church-related schools on the lower levels. It is easy to point to nations where this is done; Canada, for instance, Holland and England. What is the rationale of a government's doing so? It seems to be as simple as two plus two: the children need an education, the nation requires attendance at schools, and some of the people want their children educated in church-related schools. England, to take one example, has been furnishing immense help to church-related and other private schools, and the aim is un-doubtedly to cover the triple purpose just mentioned: to meet the needs of children and the nation, and to allow freedom of choice in education. The careful study[1] by Benjamin Sacks' on the religious issue in the state schools of England and Wales reports that, after many variations of state support for religious schools ever since 1833, in

[1] Benjamin Sacks, *The Religious Issue in the State Schools of England and Wales, 1902–1914* (University of New Mexico Press, 1961).

1958 there were in England 1,321,310 students in church-related, tax-supported schools (34% of the total number of students in all schools). Disarming and also realistic is F. H. Drinkwater's report entitled "School Aid in England" (*Commonweal*, Oct. 6, 1961).

What sort and amount of grant do the church-related schools receive in England? There is no secret about this. The amount of the grant, as Dr. Sacks shows, has varied many times since its beginning in 1833; and even since the well-known Education Act of 1944, the amount varies according as the school chooses to be merely "aided" and not to be what is called "controlled." For instance, in 1944 Roman Catholics chose to have their schools merely "aided," which meant that these schools received 90% of maintenance and 50% for replacement and expansion (this latter figure has now been increased to 75%). It may be of some interest to note that the subtitle of Dr. Sacks' interesting research work is "A Nation's Quest for Human Dignity."

As everyone knows, the Anglican Church is the national "established" church in England, and it would be curious as well as challenging if schools of non-established churches—such as the Methodist and the Roman Catholic—were freer in England, in spite of there being an established church, than are church-related schools in the United States, where there is disestablishment and state-church separation. Perhaps they are freer, if by "freer" we mean that they are in a better position to do topnotch work, have a better chance to remain viable, and are less worried and harassed by fear of financial collapse. In England, it would seem that the church-related schools are also in a more favorable position than are ours in the matter of teacher training, since in England the state, seemingly keenly aware that teachers are important, maintains training colleges for teachers in church-related schools as well as for those in other schools. For instance, as of 1962, England was said to have half a dozen state-supported teachers' training colleges for Catholic teachers, and had agreed that during 1964 it would open yet another. All of this it does (one may suppose) for the dual purpose outlined above; namely, because it is willing to go along with freedom of choice in education, since some people want their children in church-related schools, and secondly because such schools serve an essential public function.

Colleges and Universities, Yes! Schools, No!

With us in the United States, colleges and universities receive a vast amount of federal money, and as a rule this has been on an outright basis, not on a matching basis. Most of it is given for purposes of specified research, but the decisive point in the present context is that it is ordinarily given, without a shadow of discrimination, to public institutions and private ones, church-related included. Take an instance at hand, that of Notre Dame University, which is church-related. In the fiscal year 1961, for sponsored research and educational programs, Notre Dame University, like many a private institution, received federal aid. From the federal government, it received the following amounts:

from

Atomic Energy Commission	$714,410
Department of the Air Force	15,918
Department of the Army	150,491
Department of the Navy	376,704
National Institutes of Health	232,999

National Science Foundation	693,140
Office of Education	48,953
Peace Corps	3,271
total	$2,235,886

The size of the grants, which ran appreciably higher for 1962 (in fact, to more than three million), is irrelevant to our point, since the fact of the grants yields a principle and establishes a policy. The sum given to any church-related college or university is given for a specific purpose, and it is given for higher learning. This is plain. In using the money, the institution is serving a public purpose. That, too, is plain. But to say or intimate that a church-related high school or primary school serves no public purpose is to say or intimate what is patently false; if it does not, it should not be—as it is—officially approved for the education of children. And to say, as is sometimes said, that the higher institution, in doing research, is not inculcating religious values on a sectarian basis—Catholic, for instance, or Jewish or Presbyterian—is false.

We must come back in another context to these sophistic arguments, since they are helping to create a new and subsidiary myth and a nation cannot afford the luxury of myths built on falsehood. For the present, it is enough to indicate that each of the arguments is false: first, the argument based on the assumption that the higher but not the lower institution is serving a public purpose, and, secondly, the argument based on the assumption that the church-related college or university or research institute does not do a church-related work, Jewish or Christian.

The third type of aid given to private educational institutions is in the form of loans. The federal government is today making many loans to private colleges and universities, including church-related ones, often for various research purposes, as was said, and also quite readily for housing facilities. In this regard, an interesting event occurred in the spring of 1961. Abraham Ribicoff, then Secretary of Health, Education and Welfare, was busy day and night—and, it was rumored, all through the night—along with Attorney General Kennedy and a host of co-workers searching for sure and final proof that loans to church-related schools on the lower levels would most certainly be unconstitutional, though at the very moment church-related colleges and universities were seeking and obtaining large federal loans. It was like not letting your right hand know what your left hand does. Significantly, the published statements of those men's findings,[2] resting on Justice Black's position in *Everson*, was a disappointment. (As we have noted, Mr. Ribicoff who, up to that time, stood pat, at least in word, with the Administration on "no aid to schools," later revealed that he personally had always held that some aids to church-related schools are good public policy and can be constitutional.)

The convincing argument that government loans may be made to private educational institutions is the fact that these loans are made to them, and that fact should be an open book to everybody. It is obvious also that the loans are an aid to private and church-related institutions; if they were not an aid, no institution would avail itself of them. Accordingly, the two questions may be dismissed together, the question of the fact of aid being given and that of its presumed permissibility. Here we seem to have encountered questions that are closed.

[2] "Memorandum on the Impact of the First Amendment to the Constitution upon Federal Aid to Education and Welfare." Senate Document No. 29, 87th Congress, First Session (1961).

Loans to Students

Up to this point we have been considering only loans to educational institutions. Loans to students are feasible, too, and are very much in operation. Four-year scholarship loans are made, for instance, to needy undergraduates under the National Defense Education Act, and fifty per cent of the loan is cancelled—"forgiven" is the word—if, but only if, the recipient becomes a teacher in a public primary school, "public" signifying what we must regard at once as a shortsighted educational policy and as a discriminatory provision which some national congressmen have been making valiant efforts to delete. Also the Administration asked in 1962 for fifty million dollars a year to furnish loans to 212,000 additional needy undergraduates, and in this instance it was not proposed to draw any line against students attending either the public or the private colleges of the students' choice. Thirdly, immense help was proposed in Congress in 1963 to medical schools and medical and dental students; no distinction in favor or disfavor of public or private schools was contemplated; and the bill was passed and signed in this "across the board" form.

The actual or projected loans to which we refer are federal. The first effect of loans is that they help the student, and not the school; and all concede that the state as well as the federal government is competent to make loans with student aid as its primary purpose. Nevertheless, the main preoccupation of government in making loans should be and no doubt is the common good and a public purpose; for example, to enlist more and better teachers on one level or another, or to provide more and better medical service. The loans projected by the Administration to over two hundred thousand college students as well as the loans now available to medical and dental students would serve a public good and would at the same time financially aid students. Incidentally, the loans to students would indirectly aid colleges, including any church-related colleges patronized by those students; and for some suffering private colleges the help might be a windfall and make the difference between survival and death. All of which is to say that the ends achieved or to be achieved are multiple, helping the student, the public and, finally and indirectly, the patronized public or private institution.

It is obvious that a school, whatever its type or level, can be indirectly aided in both a financial and an academic way by government loans made to students; this would be the case when, for example, because of government aid, more and better students and perhaps better paying students would come to it. This helping can accrue to either a private or a public school, whatever the level; for example, when the Armed Forces send children to a private school, with the government paying their way; and the aid is unquestionably permissible. However, to aid a school is not and may not be the primary aim and purpose of any action by the State, but to help the child and the nation.

At this point, a common though minor misconception needs to be disposed of. People sometimes think it is terrifying, un-American and unconstitutional for government to be helping a private school. The fact is that a school of any kind is only an instrument, and when we help it in any way we are really helping its students and the common good. Schools have no right to exist, and have no actual existence, aside from the ends they serve; they are service centers. Therefore, "to help a school" is an ambiguous and misleading phrase. We merely repeat the thought of great philosophers such as Plato and Thomas Aquinas when we remark that teachers also have only an instrumental function in school: they help students. The conclusion is simple and commonplace. It is that we help our children and our future citizens and the national good when we help teachers and schools on any level.

As for loans to students, there are endless ways of making these and endless reasons for doing so. It may be to protect and promote health, to replenish the teacher supply, or to produce more engineers or better educated scientists or young men and women equipped to enter foreign service. But no matter what the particular end is, the State is always aiming at a public good, and if this good is served, the State which wants and needs that service performed might consider whether it should make itself ready—as it repeatedly has done—to support those being fitted to perform these public functions, and with no confession of faith required. We have already noted that our present point has been officially made by the highest court. As we have already said, the Supreme Court settled the matter in the District of Columbia case of *Bradfield v. Roberts* (1899), the logic of which comes to this: the government was in effect helping to support a hospital while the hospital performed a public function that the government needed and wanted performed. In *Bradfield*, the Court said that, in order to get its work done, the government might employ competent persons or groups without the least regard to their religious affiliation. At the same time, of course, the government might be inadvertently aiding a particular religion. The State may likewise employ a private school or other private institution to get a public work done.

A parallel situation is encountered when a city furnishes traffic policemen in front of a busy church. Every day during the peak hours, policemen aid people in traffic in front of St. Peter's Church in Chicago. They are doing what city government is bound to do—namely, look to the public good—though concurrently the city is helping persons to get to and from church and helping a particular Catholic church. In the circumstances, the city is in fact aiding a religion, and if it did not do so, it would be unable to fulfill its own public function. The city is thereby meeting to the letter the stipulation carefully worded by Justice Frankfurter's separate opinion in *McGowan v. Maryland* (1961): "Neither the National Government nor, under the Due Process Clause of the Fourteenth Amendment, a state, may, by any device, support belief or the expression of belief *for its own sake*."[3] The government proceeds to do its public, common-good work; and in doing this, it often does support belief.

In his opinion on the same occasion—*McGowan v. Maryland*—Justice Frankfurter made, with great care and precision, the point that separation or non-establishment forbids government action directed toward the primary end of affirming or promoting religious teachings. On the other hand, wrote Justice Frankfurter, "not every regulation, some of whose practical effects may facilitate the observance of a religion by its adherents, affronts the requirements of church-state separation."

Why do we cite these matters from practice and court

---

[3] Emphasis added. Concurring in *Everson*, Justice Frankfurter had declared for "absolute separation," but his 1961 statement is much more circumspect, as is his statement in this same case that American law and the Constitution merely require the implementing of "other substantial interests than the promotion of belief."

decisions relative to such matters as hospitals, city traffic, and the facilitating of religious observance? For two reasons; first, because they illustrate what the courts have said and what the various states and cities perpetually do, and, secondly, because what is done in these matters relative to hospitals and churches and "observance" or worship may be done and actually is at times done relative to students and schools.

National Science Foundation and G.I. Scholarships

Relative to students, government procedure is seen, for example, in some of the work done by the National Science Foundation.[4] The N.S.F. has several functions, one of which is to give money to universities, including church-related ones, with the stipulation that the money be used *to improve high school teaching* in subjects such as mathematics, chemistry and modern languages, the public purpose in the case being an effort to meet the problem so sharply posed by Sputnik. What the N.S.F. exists and operates for is manifest; it is not primarily for the good of the benefited university, the good of the high school teacher or student or the high schools actually benefited, but to serve a public good. To repeat Justice Frankfurter's well chosen words, the government may not aid a church-related university "for its own sake." This was his way of saying that the government's first aim must be a public good. It does not aim to benefit any church, any university or any high school, public or private. But it does in effect benefit many a university and many a high school, and in benefiting a

[4] Within the National Defense Act of 1958.

church-related university or high school, it may chance to benefit a particular religion. It would be unreasonable if the N.S.F. had to make an inquisition into the faith of persons or institutions thus benefited. Well provided with the taxpayer's money, the N.S.F. benefits the selected university, church-related or other, and also the high school and its students, whatever their faith, and the individual teacher, whatever his faith and whatever the public or the private high school he comes from or returns to serve. No religious test is made. Each summer since 1958, a particular Catholic university[5] had four hundred high school teachers, most of them Catholic, but some Protestant, including Protestant ministers, studying in order to become better prepared teachers of high school mathematics, thanks to an N.S.F. grant. Those students were given no money, but, happily for them, they paid no money; their financial way was clear, thanks to the same grant. They were academically better off, their church-related schools were academically better off, and the church-related university in question was financially and perhaps academically better off. While the federal government was thus serving the urgent public purpose, the church-related teachers and the church-related university and high schools might also be legally and constitutionally served out of the taxpayer's generous pocket. That is the way freedom works in a pluralist and democratic society, and all of this is quite in line with the multiple-purpose idea and likewise with the decision rendered in *Bradfield v. Roberts*.

That is typical of what is always going on; life is too complicated, and our belief in religious and other freedoms

[5] For the sake of the discussion, Notre Dame University.

too strong, to demand a declaration of faith from this or that group when we want a public work done. The aim of the N.S.F. in other instances is better teaching in physics and chemistry and modern languages, and all citizens see that this aim, as an item under the public and national good, should on occasion be the object of national concern and national spending. Let us repeat: particular students are thereby aided, as are their high schools, some of which are church-related; and also aided are the church-related universities they attend, though the aid to high schools and universities, whatever their faith, is not, to reiterate Justice Frankfurter's stipulation, for their own sake. It would be unreasonable as well as discriminatory if, in spending for the needed public good, we felt constrained to draw the line against high schools and against their students and teachers because of affiliation with one or another religious faith. Such discrimination would violate the "no interference" clause of the First Amendment; the State would be requiring a profession of faith from those to whom it gave assistance so that they could better serve the public good.

Or again take the operation of that best-known experience, the G.I. Bill of Rights, itself so much like the working of those N.S.F. grants made to universities of all types and, through them, to a multitude of teachers and students on the high school level. The G.I. Bill drew no faith or color lines as to students or schools and no lines as to academic levels. Whatever their faith, the students were helped, and it was theirs freely to choose schools on any level and for any sort of studies. They attended colleges and universities, but they also attended high schools, culinary schools, barber schools, and so forth, and, if they wished, grade schools. The religious faith of the student or school was entirely out of the question; so was the level, high or low, of the student's choice; and so, too, was the public or the private character of the school attended. And the G.I. Bill worked extraordinarily well, with all its freedom, causing no conflict or animosities, no hardship on students or schools of any type, and no interference with faith or freedom.

It is often said that this G.I. schooling was a sort of back-pay and bonus, and perhaps it was, both in intention and in fact. At the same time, government might engage in it only as serving a public good, and, whatever may have been anyone's intentions, the practice served the private good of persons and of schools. It is, all over again, the dual- or triple-purpose idea: at one stroke the State is able to achieve several good ends, one of which is public, primary and direct, and the others are private and foreseen and by no means precluded.

Let us consider for a moment what might be the common-sense conclusion from the experience with G.I. and N.S.F. grants. By analogy with them we might make out a strong case for some government support of students attending private educational institutions on any and all levels. These institutions exist and operate all over the nation and are the product of a free development by the people, and the State should at least smile on this beneficent working of freedom. They do a public work which needs to be done and, in that sense, are public. And because state-sponsored schools on all levels are overloaded with work, the State is in a poor position today, and will probably be in a poor position for a long time to come, to do all of this needed public work.

If anyone objects that the State, aiding church-related lower schools, would be aiding particular religions, we would say *a*) that this need not be an evil thing to do, *b*) that the State does so all the time, anyway, *c*) that its aim, if it is a worthy state, would be the common public good, and *d*) that it could, as is done—for instance, in Canada—*pay only to the parents or children and never directly to the school.*

We repeat that private educational institutions on all levels are in fact doing a public work that needs to be done. Therefore the State, no doubt wanting such a work done, anxious to bless freedoms, and yet itself scarcely in a position to do the work, might well begin to seek feasible ways to encourage and assist those who do the work on a freedom basis. Otherwise the State might appear, on the one hand, indifferent to a public good and, on the other, a bit like a sponge. For the State merely to stand by and tolerate someone's doing this important work that the State needs to have done is, we suggest, far from the level of equity.

A dual objection is sometimes made to the proposal that some aid be given to private schools, especially on the lower levels. The objection is that sects would then multiply schools and thus draw off some tax aid from public lower schools and thereby really hurt these schools. To this we reply, first, that sectarian schools indeed might multiply; and yet at least American private and sectarian institutions of higher learning have not done so when they have received notable aid, and English private lower schools, given aid, have actually declined proportionately and numerically. And we reply, secondly, that public schools on the lower levels, aided out of all proportion to any aid ever given to private schools, should be able and anxious to stand up to this modicum of competition. To concede that they could not would be to concede that they are mismanaged.

Page Boys Privately Educated

In concluding this question of freedom in the area of student scholarships, we shall briefly consider the instance of the page boys in the federal Congress. These boys, who should be selected without regard to creed or color, are given scholarships to schools chosen by the boys and their parents. The result is that they may go, if they wish, to church related or other private schools, with the taxpayer footing their bills. It would be difficult to see why they and their parents should not have this freedom of choice, and we could scarcely find a separationist so unreasonable and reactionary as to deny it to them.

The pages' receiving the scholarships and enjoying freedom of choice is a matter of slight importance in itself. But the practice means the acceptance of a principle and seems to set a pattern: some American youths on the high school level are receiving federal scholarships and are free to use them at any American schools of their choice. If the page boys may receive scholarships to church-related schools—as some of the boys do—then there is presumably nothing in the Constitution against federal-grant scholarships to students attending high schools of any type. It is permissible to spend federal money to finance a youth's high school education in any type of school—that is the implication of this well-accepted practice, unless, that is, the practice of granting these scholarships is unconstitutional and against the separation principle in the first place, and yet one would waste his time trying to find a dozen persons outside the American Civil Liberties Union to challenge the practice. The page boys are not un-American and are not more American than their brothers and sisters or than the neighbors' children.

The Cosmic Leap into College

The instance of the page boys is sufficient, even by itself, to suggest that scholarships may be given to students in all types of schools on the lower levels. But we may go a step farther. The G.I. Bill, which was much more democratic than are page-boy scholarships, allowed scholarships in regular high schools and grade schools and in trade schools of any variety and on any level. We underline the point because there is unnecessary confusion about it, even among some experts and in high places. President Kennedy, to take merely one name, repeatedly, if perhaps rather arbitrarily, said that tax-money loans and scholarships are perfectly permissible on the college and university levels but are to be rigidly refused for constitutional, First Amendment reasons on the primary and secondary levels.

In this connection, the favoring or disfavoring of school levels is meaningless. We refer to scholarships to any school of the students' choice, since, to carry their case through, opponents of aid to students in church-related schools would have to show that both the G.I. and the page-boy scholarships are unconstitutional, and no one is likely to attempt to do that.

But people would have to do far more than show the unconstitutionality of G.I. and page-boy scholarships. They would have to show a basic constitutional reason for allowing loans and scholarships on the college and university levels, for instance to engineering, medical and dental students and prospective teachers, and a basic contrary constitutional disqualification of loans and scholarships on the lower levels. This they will find very difficult to do. The reason is that there is no basis in the Constitution for such a distinction. Recall that Secretary Ribicoff and Attorney General Robert Kennedy had a core of workers looking, day and night, back and forth through the Constitution and Supreme Court decisions, and they found no compelling constitutional distinction between aid to high school students and aid to college students.

The problem for anyone holding to a decisive constitutional gap between high school and college students is to show that there is something constitutionally different between a high school senior and a college freshman. This would be an arduous and unrewarding task since, in reality, there is no such constitutional difference.

The position to which we are presently objecting is that there is a constitutional allowance for federal grants or loans to private and church-related colleges, but no such allowance for grants or loans to religious schools. Arguments to favor grants or loans on the higher levels though denying them on the lower were adduced in the "Memorandum on the Impact of the First Amendment to the Constitution upon Federal Aid to Education and Welfare."[6] These were the arguments adduced: 1) Private institutions play a much greater role in higher than in primary and secondary education. 2) State colleges and universities cannot take care of all wanting higher education. 3) No one is required to attend college. 4) The State provides tuition-free education at the lower levels. 5) Religion is less a feature of church-related colleges than of church-related primary schools. 6) The college student, being more mature, is less open to sectarian indoctrination.

A second look at numbers one and two might raise

[6] Senate Document No. 29, 87th Congress, First Session, pp. 5, 24–26.

serious doubts and questions, and, of course, number three—that all are required to go to school and none required to go to college—is out of place and is really an argument, not for the support of those choosing to attend college, but for the support of parents who must send their children to school.

Another consideration stands in favor of the college side of the argument. It is that, even in the church-related college or university, both the student body and the faculty are religiously far more mixed than in the lower schools. In favor of aid to the schools, Professor Kauper adds two points: first, that the religious schools "do serve a secular as well as a religious purpose" and, second, "that the state in giving some assistance to parochial schools is thereby making a meaningful contribution in support of the right of parents to send children to the school of their choice."[7]

By great efforts, therefore, it is possible to make out a half-convincing argument for one side as against the other: to favor aid—if aid of any sort is to be given—for the lower levels, or for the higher levels. The strongest argument so far adduced to favor one level as against the other is on the side of the lower levels, since parents are obliged to send their children to lower schools whereas nobody is legally obliged to attend colleges or universities. But constitutionally—supposing our premise to be the Constitution—there is no ground for a distinction between grade school and college. There is not a word in the Constitution to suggest such a statement as "At the freshman level in college, tax-paid loans and scholarships shall begin; but no sooner." There is no basis in the Constitution for any such distinc-

[7] Paul G. Kauper, *Civil Liberties and the Constitution* (Ann Arbor: University of Michigan Press, 1962), p. 50.

tion. Professor Harry W. Jones, of the University of Chicago Law School, said at the Chicago Institute of 1963: "No conceivable Congress would ever authorize financial aid to all private colleges *except* those having church affiliations. But I am not at all sure that the widely accepted distinction between aid to schools and aid to colleges is one that can be justified in terms of constitutional principle." Arguments to show a constitutional gap between high school and college rest either on political and religious expediency or on confusion. Is anyone so naïve as to think that something is said in the Constitution about the difference between the high school and the college student? This burgeoning myth should be destroyed.

We are not at the moment arguing that there should or should not be loans and scholarships on one level or the other, but only saying that if taxpayer loans and scholarships are constitutional for college and university students, they are exactly as constitutional, not more and not less, for grade and high school students. President Kennedy and former Secretary Ribicoff and Secretary Celebrezze held to a distinction which has no basis in fact or reason. What is constitutionally good for students and schools on one level is good for those on another level. Only political or religious interests would attempt to hold otherwise.

The expediency base of the argument showed through in a study document. This was a quite formal and serious report received in 1963 by the National Lutheran Council. The report declared for government aid to college education, but against aid at lower levels—because, said the report, tax aid to lower levels would help some religious groups more than others. Evidently the argument in this instance rested on expediency and not on constitutional principles or on the educational good of children or the common good. One is happy to note that the report was eventually rejected.

One, Two, Three

Our argument from preceding chapters and up to this point holds together in the following way. First, religious schools are and have always been a part of the American educational enterprise, and are legally and officially declared to be such. Second, these schools, whatever their level, serve a public purpose. Third, there is and always has been much collaboration between Church and State, and the presumption is that at least some of it is constitutional. In any event, it is much too late in the day to go back and try to invalidate the words and practices of Washington and Jefferson and their many successors. Fourth, there is and always has been aid given in many forms to church-related schools, and again the presumption is that at least some of it, given today or in the past, is constitutional. Fifth, the wedge technique—the attempt to drive a wedge between the high school student and the college student—is, when scrutinized, seen to rest on nothing more substantial than political or theological expediency and Machiavellianism.

An excellent summary of these many matters was, happily for us, made in a 1962 talk by a distinguished spiritual leader who is also a distinguished historian of education. In Rodeph Shalom Synagogue, Philadelphia, William W. Brickman, of New York University, made these points:

If separation, as Mr. Justice Frankfurter stated, means separation and nothing else, then it can be said that there never was a Church-State separation in the United States, especially in education.

There are numerous examples throughout our history of Federal and state aid to denominational schools and colleges. At the present time there are numerous religious schools which are enjoying the benefits of loans for improving instruction in science, mathematics and languages under the National Defense Act of 1958.

Isn't the principle of separation equally applicable to loans as to grants, to religious schools as to colleges? Yet no one in government, including the President, has made any determined effort to be consistent. Why not?

Because there was no intention in our history to institute a complete separation. But if separation is not complete, it is not separation.

Dr. Brickman concluded by saying that his fellow Jews had been far too long "one-sidedly devoted to a dubious doctrine of separationism."

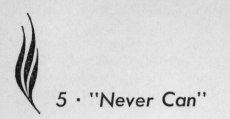

5 · "Never Can"

Absolute Separation

Our next point, following naturally on the five points summarized a moment ago, refers not to a constitutional question at all, but to a state of mind, and yet, odd though it might at first appear, in practice this is a matter as weighty and decisive as the constitutional matter. In brief, it is this: those who say, "No collaboration between Church and State; never, under any circumstances," are absolutists. So, too, for those who say, "Never, under any circumstances; no collaboration between the State and church-related schools; no aid in any form or measure to students in those schools, or to parents sending children to church-related schools." It is expecting much to ask anyone to discuss the problem with these people, since in this context they tend to have closed minds. To everything and anything one might say, their reply is abrupt and final, and is given in the word "Separation!" Though these people plainly are absolutists, we pass no judgment on their goodness or badness. What we refer to is their cast of mind, and at the same time we must concede that society will always have some persons of this type.

They tend to all or nothing. On the school question, they tend to all this or all that, to declare for public schools only—only these are worthy of consideration. They would allow no support in any form or degree for private schools, or they would demand total support for private schools. They may well be of a simplistic and naïve turn of mind, and some might be like one-track minds. For them, there are no two sides to the question, since, to begin with, the question is closed. Naturally, it is difficult for them to take an intelligent part in social and political affairs which, in general, require many nuances. They suffer radical and as if congenital difficulty with pluralist theory and practice, and they would unconsciously turn democracy into a body of dogmas and absolutes. People of this type are found in each of the four major faiths.

This "state of mind" has great influence on the question of education. The notion of an absolute separation in America between Church and State is as if self-evident to many minds, and so too for the notion of an absolute separation between the State and the church-related school. They take "separation" to mean absolute separation, and the fact that we have had a century and a half of collaboration between Church and State is meaningless to them, since they are so sure a priori that there is absolute separation. The slogan or shibboleth *separation* has thus become a first principle with them, and they deduce everything from it. All questions are triumphantly met in advance, and the absolutist has his answer on the tip of his tongue in the one word *separation*.

There are many current instances of this a priori and dogmatic mind. In 1963, a study called "Public Funds for

Parochial Schools" was brought out by the National Council of Churches. This Protestant body makes no bones about aid to church-related hospitals, whether Jewish, Catholic or Protestant, or to Jewish, Catholic and Protestant churches, or again about aid to church-related colleges, many of which are Protestant. But beyond that point, it draws the line and begins using the word separation in a dogmatic and absolute sense. It affirms that the use of tax funds for religious schools on the lower levels "would undermine our historical ideal of separation of church and state." The argument comes to this: aid and no separation where this reading helps us; separation and no aid where there is a question of others.

The mere word *separation* is made at once a crutch, a shield and a banner.

Interesting also were the reactions, mostly on the strength of the word *separation*, of some congressmen in Iowa. In 1963, the Methodist governor of that state suggested to his congress that bus service be made available to all school children, and some congressmen were interviewed. Said one: "I think the bus position is a clear breach of separation of Church and State under the Federal as well as our State Constitution." Said another: "Absolutely not. No mixing of Church and State." And a third: "Once the Church-State thing gets breached, you can't tell where to draw the line."

These good and worthy congressmen ignored historical and present-day contexts within which Church and State in Iowa and elsewhere have worked and do now work so amicably and so extensively together. Yet in their incantation of "separation, separation," they were probably as innocent and candid as the sun.

In other words, men and groups can be absolutists without knowing it. The word *separation* has been turned into something like a rhythmic prayer. To men such as those congressmen, historical and current facts would be uncongenial and would slip off their minds.

Next, take some top-level illustrations of absolutists. The famous official statements on Church and State alleging absolute separation and non-collaboration are those of Justice Black in the *Everson* and *McCollum* cases. What he said in the first case (1947), Mr. Black repeated in the second (1948). As noted above, this is what he said: "Neither a state nor the Federal Government can set up a church. Neither can pass laws which aid one religion, aid all religions, or prefer one religion over another. . . . No tax in large or small can be levied to support any religious activities or institutions. . . . The clause against establishment was intended to erect a wall." This was strong, and Justice Rutledge made separation yet stronger when, dissenting in *Everson*, he said of the First Amendment: "The Amendment's purpose was not to strike merely at the official establishment of a single sect, creed or religion, outlawing only a formal relation such as had prevailed in England and some of the colonies. Necessarily it was to uproot all such relationships. But the object was broader than separating church and state in that narrow sense. It was to create a complete and permanent separation of the spheres of religious activity and civil authority by comprehensively forbidding every form of public aid or support for religion."

Those classical statements are full of adamant and absolute dicta: "neither-nor," "to strike at," "to outlaw," "to uproot all such," "to create a complete and permanent separation," "to erect a wall."

The trouble with the absolutist position is that it is

unreal, unhistorical and unworkable, and has always been outside of American experience. It takes little account either of history or of the pluralist character of our institutions, for, as we have shown at length, there has never been a total and absolute separation, but in reality much close co-operation between Church and State, in the United States. Justice Douglas expressed our position in a mild manner in the *Zorach* case, when, having noted that the State may not compel any form of religious observance, he continued: "This does not, however, prevent all co-operation between Church and State." In short, there is some cooperation, and on this issue absolutism is out of the picture.

Even if we wanted to, it would be impossible at this late date to change our past or even to teach the old American dog new tricks. To make us desist, now, from our American ways would require the energy and daring of a strong-armed totalitarian ruler. Of course, we will always have absolutists among us, the unbending, the all-or-nothing cast of mind. What is important, however, is to see that the never-never and absolutist approach to social problems in general and to Church-State relations and Church-State-school relations is totally out of line with American history and contemporary practice and a misfit for the American pattern. Total separation would be both poor theory and bad because unworkable in practice.

We could hardly repeat too often that an uncompromising absolutism, though it has been affirmed by some men on the highest court, is useless in the everyday operation of the national educational enterprise. Odd it is, too, that the position has been tenaciously clung to by others besides Justices Black and Rutledge. Once upon a time, Justice Frankfurter made a strong declaration for absolutism in the relations of Church and State, and by this time in our history one might, on rereading *Everson*, be shocked to see that in 1947 Justice Frankfurter took the First Amendment as an absolute. In that famous case, parents, it was agreed, might be reimbursed for bus fares paid to carry their children to parochial schools. The basis of the decision was that, because the bus service protected and aided the child, the reimbursing was constitutional. It seems that Justice Frankfurter was considerably troubled by the decision, for, speaking of it, he said: "We find that the basic constitutional principle of absolute separation was violated."

The question is whether there is a principle of "absolute separation," and we are happy to repeat again and again that Justice Frankfurter appears to have rescinded that absolute position. If he has done so, others have not. *The New York Times*, adamant and absolutist on one side of the First Amendment and skipping the other side, has continued to affirm separation as absolute. In an editorial (March 16, 1961) the *Times* spoke of "those who believe as we do in the absolute separation of church and state in accordance with the New York Constitution." Whatever of the legal demands in New York or any other state, "absolute separation" is, in the face of American practice, a somewhat extreme view, the editors seeing only one side of the question and thus seeing this side out of perspective. As the editors of *America* have remarked, the *Times* editors seem to have "a bad case of parochial school jitters." Even with regard to the National Defense Education Act, which, for a public purpose—namely, to improve the teaching and learning of mathematics, science and foreign languages, and to keep up in the space age—has authorized grants to public schools though only loans to private schools, a *Times* editorial (May 12, 1961) said: ". . . and we would limit the program to public schools." So, too, a lawyer for the American Civil Liberties Union declared in 1962: "I believe the wall of separation must be kept impregnable. The constitutional principle, and the need today as before, is for a complete and absolute separation." (Most lawyers for the ACLU would echo those sentiments.)

"The 'Absolutist' Construction"

Having sufficiently scolded those who cling to the absolutist theory, we must now appreciatively listen to experts on legal and constitutional history who, fortunately for us, have made it their business to say just what we have been saying. One thinks at once of Dr. Kurland, of the University of Chicago Law School; Dr. Katz, formerly of the same school and now of Wisconsin University Law School; Dr. Kauper, of Michigan University Law School; and Dr. Sutherland, of Harvard Law School. Within their scholarly studies, these and other experts indicate the forced and unnatural position of the once-for-all absolute answer. At the end of a long study (in the *University of Chicago Law Review*, Autumn 1961) of Church-State and the First Amendment—that is to say, of what he calls "the freedom and separation clauses"—Dr. Philip Kurland concludes that, whatever else, the absolutist position is false to the facts. He says that in regard to the state contributing, directly or indirectly, to parochial education, neither the ever-ever nor the never-never answer makes sense. Anyone, he maintains, who suggests that as a matter of constitutional law the answer is clear one way or the other "is either deluding or deluded." "The seeming simplicity of the 'absolutist' construction of the First Amendment is only too patently disingenuous." So says Kurland at the end of his careful study; and his main conclusion, after the consideration of many relevant legal cases, is that we are bound to respect the two clauses at once and together, and preferably as one: the freedom of religion clause and the separation or "no favoring of any church" clause. To be partial to one is to be unfair to the other.

Consider the words of another professional. For several years and in several studies, Dr. Paul G. Kauper, of Michigan Law School, has kept coming to the same conclusion as Dr. Kurland in regard to the absolutist theory, and also incidentally reminding us of Justice Holmes' observation that a page of history is worth a volume of logic. A page of history is enough to invalidate the absolutist position since "never-never" is powerless against "once upon a time." On the basis of legal and constitutional studies, Dr. Kauper's article in the *Michigan Law Review* (November 1961) made these four points relevant to Church-State and Church-State-school relations:

First, there is evidently an interdependence and collaboration of Church and State in American experience, and the attempt to rationalize this out of existence is a failure. For example, he notes that the Church advises its members to vote, to pay taxes, to serve in war and as officials, and it contributes to the State by cultivating the spiritual life; for its part, the State among other contributions protects church property and allows Jehovah Witnesses the use of sidewalks and public parks for preaching; and Church and State often work together on matters such as peace, disarmament, and food for the needy.

Second, says Dr. Kauper, Justice Black's declaration that government cannot aid religion presents a difficulty; notwithstanding Justice Black's statements in *Everson* and

McCollum, the historical fact is that government funds have often been spent and continue to be spent in support of religious purposes.

Third, concurring in the Sunday law decision (1961), Justice Frankfurter said that government can never do anything that will support or endorse religious views. History, says Dr. Kauper, is against such a sweeping assertion.

Fourth, in the *Zorach* decision (1952) the Supreme Court said that the working together of the State and religious education is one of degree, and this statement, says Dr. Kauper, may be the most significant in the entire case, since problems in the area of social and human affairs cannot be solved by resort to "doctrinaire absolutes."

In regard to those absolutes, Dr. Kauper has several times recorded his convictions. Contributing to Erich Walter's *Religion and the State University*, Dr. Kauper said: "The majority opinion in the *Zorach* case restored what appeared to many to be a sound perspective and judgment in the interpretation of the separation principle regarded as a constitutional mandate. The matter of separation cannot be approached in terms of verbal absolutes. Nor can a metaphor such as 'the wall of separation' serve as an aid to analysis. The truth is that religion and government have been and continue to be interrelated, and that by hypothesis it is impossible to describe this situation in terms of 'absolute and complete separation.' . . . The idea that the separation principle means that government cannot 'aid' religion, if stated as a universal and absolute proposition, is not supported by precedent, history, or the common understanding."[1]

[1] Paul G. Kauper, *Religion and the State University*, edited by Erich A. Walter (University of Michigan Press, 1958), p. 76.

Remarkable also is Dr. Arthur E. Sutherland's mature and beautiful article, "Due Process and Disestablishment," in the June 1949 issue of the *Harvard Law Review*, where the author says that readers in the history of Church and State must be struck by two long-standing American traditions. One is an intimate association between Church and State. The other is what he calls a symbiosis of Church and school. Each tradition has waned, and yet, says Dr. Sutherland, the tradition associating religion with education dies hard; note the invocation by the minister at most graduation exercises—which are often transferred to a Protestant church—and songs of a religious nature at Thanksgiving and Christmas, to say nothing of "America" and the "Star Spangled Banner."

After citing ways in which Church and State cooperate, Erwin R. Griswold, of Yale Law School, asks: "Must all of these things be extirpated in order to satisfy a constitutional absolutism? . . . I do not believe that the contentions now made would occur to any man who could free himself from an absolute approach to the problem."

The opinion of the legal experts has been frequently expressed in recent years, especially after and as a result of the *McCollum* decision (1948) and the Lord's Prayer case (1963). Happily, they keep the question open and in the arena of debate. At the conclusion of and as the result of a debate held in 1963, Dr. Robert McCabe, of the New York University Law School, said in regard to the constitutionality of tuition grants for pupils in religious schools: "This presents a close question, yet it seems in line with the Supreme Court's decision in the *Everson* case. Under such a view, the pupil's burden in obtaining an education may be eased and he is allowed a free choice of schools."

Two Sides to the First Amendment

There are generally two sides to a social issue, and this is notably the case with the First Amendment, in which a remarkable attempt was made to balance matters: to balance freedom on the one side with no favoritism on the other, no petting and coddling of any church on the one hand and no interfering with religious freedom on the other. To do this in practice must always prove to be difficult. The problem continues to be one of balance, and this has to be a precarious and teetering balance. Separation itself, so important to groups and persons and the nation when rightly understood and applied, would be evil if it interfered with freedom and rights. It would be evil if it interfered with the freedom and right of parents to have an effective voice in choosing where and by whom and how their children shall be educated. We say an "effective" voice, since a right that is merely on paper can be nullified without so much as being mentioned.

In the decision against the Oregon public-schools-only law (1925), it was emphasized that the parents have the primary right in education, but that the State also certainly has rights; the State having the indefeasible right to say that the normal child's education shall reach such and such a minimum—that needed for citizenship—and the parents having the unquestionable right to say where and by whom the education shall be obtained and what shall be the kind of education, including, if they wish, a religious education for their children.

But the other side of the question remains basically significant, too, and the balance must be kept: that is the genius and merit of the First Amendment. On the education issue, the other side is that we must be careful that, so far as the State itself might in any way help a church-related college or school, by whomsoever operated, the State is not thereby primarily aiming to help the religious aspects of education. The State's aim must first of all be the secular aspects of education, whether in public or private schools, and, secondly, the religious and theological aspects only insofar as they are a part of our general cultural inheritance. It must endeavor to promote the religious aspects only for a public purpose, since that good is the proper object of any action by the State. Here again the State has the difficult though not surprising or at all novel problem of trying to manage a precarious and teetering balance; and, even making its best efforts, it will always meet with complaints from special interests, those of secularists, Jews, Catholics or Protestants. The remarkable thing is that on the whole it does so well, given the facts that the problem is complicated and that in America the State has always been helping the churches.

A perpetual difficulty for the State in education is inherent in the circumstance that each of the four groups mentioned is a watchdog. Each is ready to pounce on the State and on any other of the four and to tear it to pieces. At the conferences held in New York and Chicago on Church, State and school, one notices how wary are the participants, how they are (in notable part) not inquirers at all, but partisans, and how they are blocked and almost boxed into definitely aligned groups. In a way, the wariness of each body—secularists, Jews, Catholics and Protestants—is justified. The State itself and each of these groups—and each of their inter-groupings—will no doubt bear watching, since eternal vigilance is the price of liberty.

Yet each of them is wrong, and all are wrong. As we

shall show at length in our treatment of pluralism, there is some better way to work for national educational good than for the four religions to hound each other or for the State to make the practice of religious freedom onerous. Even out of self-respect if not out of respect for justice and truth, the State and each of those four will have to learn to work with all on common educational problems. From the point of view of the most rigid and belligerent members within a group, each religion will have to appear to be a straddler and compromiser. Those religionists who still embrace the myth of an absolute separation will sooner or later have to relinquish this fiction; it was already relinquished in Washington's day and again in Jefferson's day, and no one should attempt to make it into a retroactive law now. As Robert M. Hutchins has said, the wall cannot help us to learn, and on the other hand it surely can hamper the search for a national policy of education and a national program to carry it out. Wall worship and a mere incantation of "separation" will generate no light.

To begin to create a climate in which we all might hope to work for possible solutions—which, of course, means the total and national educational good—many of us, including top-ranking churchmen and educationists, will have hard lessons to learn. All will have to learn charity, sympathy, and understanding, and this means that we must do some actual work together. We will continually have the problem of doing the truth in charity, and, in that way, of learning the truth. We must drop certain easy assumptions. We will have to get rid of the assumption that some schools or other—say, the Catholic or the public—are a world apart and have merely to struggle with their own isolated problems. In President Kennedy's fine declaration, the educational problem is not a regional one or (we suppose) a sectarian or a public-school or a private-school problem. It is an over-all national problem requiring and rightly demanding the cooperation of all men of good will. It will need vision and courage and generosity and educational statesmanship of a high order. Those who are seeking only their own good or their group's sectarian good—for instance, the good of the Catholic schools or the public schools—are severely limiting their usefulness in this important work.

Although some problems within the national complexus of problems may need to be considered almost as if alone and separate, we must, if we wish to do what has to be done, see them as parts within the national whole. Take the analogy of the integration problem. This occurs as a national and international problem, and not a problem solely in Cambridge or Birmingham, and it involves items other than color. So too of any possible aid to private and church-related schools. This is a problem, not merely of those patronizing such schools, but of all honest and patriotic men and groups concerned with education. We desire and need good schools for all, and it will take the cooperation of all to secure and maintain them.

This, then, is everybody's problem. It is first of all the parents' problem, and then the teachers' and the schools' problem, and the problem of the educational associations, and the Presidents' and the Senate's and the House's problem, and the problem of the churches and the courts. All must learn to work together, sympathetically seeking the good of each other while seeking the good of all.

In Search of Guide-Lines

We are far from attempting to make out a blueprint

and to say what is the solution of either the total national educational problem or of the problem of any allowable aid to private schools. Nevertheless we feel constrained to suggest guide-lines within which it may be possible for solutions to operate. One of the important guide-lines has been emphasized; namely, that to proclaim absolute separation is stretching things too far. This absolutism is inoperative in fact, would be far from good theory, and no flexible mind believing in democracy would want it. On the other hand, our actual collaboration between Church and State, or again between church-school or church-hospital and State, must continue to be one of the most delicate tests of belief in freedom and pluralist democracy.

Trouble recurrently arises from the complexity of the First Amendment and from the fact that some are sure to claim too much, and some likely to obtain too little. This is not an abstract declaration; among others, Jews and Catholics often have had their freedoms somewhat narrowed. This is the strenuous life—attempting to maintain a balance between the two parts of the Amendment. No wonder the process requires and deserves surveillance by sharp even if reasonable watchdogs.

All these persons and all these groups—that is one thing; another is the freedoms, including religious freedom, and this freedom balanced with no favoritism. All of this demands care and vigilance, and only a somewhat simple mind would assume that the problem would some day dissolve and vanish. Of course, there is one obvious easy way— the appeal to absolutes, although that is perfectly useless in the hard knocks of everyday practice.

Take the freedom side, which, even by itself, is delicate and complex. People are free to found and operate schools on a private, non-state basis, and parents are free to send their children to such schools, some of which may be church-related. Teamed with this freedom is the freedom of parents to bring up children in the religion of the parents. That is the freedom arrangement which we all want, and it is an arrangement blest officially by the Constitution. But it might seem that this freedom could be attenuated and even destroyed by conditions. It could be destroyed by a heavy tax to support public schools only, and then progressively by more and more local, state and federal taxes to support public schools only. Evidently this would be freedom with a price tag on it. For, under such circumstances, to exercise freedom to send children to religious schools would become increasingly burdensome, and for many parents it might become impossible. The upshot would be that support exclusively for public schools would be like a law requiring all to attend public schools. Something would have happened to make freedom of choice in education disappear. The freedom side of the First Amendment would unduly suffer and in practice would tend to be nullified.

Is this a result that we are anxious to promote? Before we do so, we should think carefully. For one thing, we might notice the declarations of Representative Hugh L. Carey, of New York, to Congress. What he has said falls into two parts. First, that it is "neither practical nor economical to price out, phase out, in effect drop out, an entire school system." Second, economy "should mean the maximum utilization of every existing school and classroom which meets state and local standards, public or private." As stated by the Congressman, these are serious questions of national policy and are obviously practical.

Within a scholarly context, Professor Kurland has said that the "wall" has been built up to protect us in both directions: first, against any favorite or established church and, secondly, in the exercise of religious freedom. Support for only one type of school would be tantamount to an effective attack on the freedom of religion clause.

The American way, right or wrong, has always been to aid religious schools. Nevertheless, this is a knotty problem. It would be only too easy to begin favoring, no matter in what form and in what covert ways and to what extent. There is no doubt that in regard to schools the aid and comfort have historically been on the side of Protestantism, and still are markedly on that side, above all in the Deep South, but also at places in the North. In his study called *The School Bus Law*, Theodore Powell reported that for some Protestants in Connecticut, Church-State separation primarily meant prohibition of public financial aid or services for parochial schools, but almost never meant prohibition of the use of public schools for the promotion of religion; in one area, Protestants saw dental aid to parochial school students as unconstitutional, "but voted in favor of the distribution of Gideon Bibles in the public schools." In Powell's summary, "separation" was used against Catholic aspirations, and "cooperation" of Church, State and school in favor of Protestant desires. To keep the First Amendment balance is thus seen to be extremely difficult even today in New England; and the 1963 Supreme Court decision against the use of the Lord's Prayer and the Bible as a part of religious exercises in public schools may be viewed as a further installment on the disestablishment of Protestant churches in American public schools; as Walter Lippmann noted, we should look on the decision as merely an official declaration that trying to pressure religious exercises into public schools is like trying to make our way through a blind alley. Thus the decision makes more urgent the need to do whatever is allowable to aid students in religious-orientated schools.

An applicable criterion can be found as to when and where and under what conditions and to what extent to furnish aid. Any aid has to be kept within two guide-lines. The first is that aid, if there is to be aid, has—as already re-marked—to be primarily for a public good, since that is the only purpose for which tax money may ever be used, in the case of schools or anything else. As we have said, only on the ground of serving a public function may the public school receive the aid it perpetually receives; and the same criterion must be used if any aid is extended to any type of private school. That criterion was used when, during Washington's presidency, federal money was made available to Christian missions among Indians, not primarily for a religious work, but, as the rescript emphasized, for the happiness and peace of the Indians and their attachment to the United States. The government breached no wall then in furnishing aid for a public purpose, and it would not need to breach any wall now in serving a public purpose and the common good of the nation, while protecting freedom of choice in education. It would no more breach a wall in thus aiding a public purpose than it does in furnishing chaplains to the military or to Congress or in effectively furnishing scholarships to teachers of high school science and mathematics.

This point was well expressed, at least in part, by a Lutheran educator, Dr. W. A. Poehler, president of Concordia College in Minnesota. In 1963, Dr. Poehler said: "I don't see where the wall is going to be breached by granting children free lunch at noon, a glass of milk and a ride to school."

The second criterion or guide-line would be that any

aid to religious schools should be furnished only for what may be called a secular end; for instance, for the safety and health of the children, as was done in the *Everson* bus decision (1947), or for their secular education, as was done in the *Cochran* secular-textbook case (1930), in which the Supreme Court decreed that the State may spend money for textbooks used in secular subjects, in either private-parochial or public schools. The same criterion manifestly holds for furnishing polio shots and milk and hot lunches to children regardless of the approved public or private school their parents may choose to have them attend.

Bus service, textbooks in secular areas, lunches and polio shots are among the easier instances, or at least they should always be so considered by those concerned for the child's welfare and the public good. They fall within what is called "the child benefit theory." However, beyond such instances we encounter perplexing questions. Take the following as possible cases.

First. The AFL-CIO executive council has urged that any federal aid to education bill should include students in independent primary and secondary schools with "as much assistance as is constitutionally possible." The statement expresses great good will, but the question is whether this kind of criterion would be of any use in determining how much and in which ways, if any at all, to aid those students.

Second. Because their schools are independent in a pluralist and freedom-loving society, and because their schools perform a public service, Rabbi Alexander Mittlemann, of Rochester, N.Y., has declared that students in independent schools "deserve public support on the local, state and national level *as far as their general curriculum is concerned.*" We emphasize the Rabbi's concluding words as expressing a very interesting and perhaps usable criterion.

Third. In Missouri, a recently passed tax-supported program offers special education for handicapped children, notably those with speech and hearing problems, the teacher-specialists traveling from school to school within the area, and drawing no line of favor or disfavor for public schools or independent schools, with, in fact, approximately 5,000 students in parochial and other independent schools being served. Is this Missouri program an instance of breaching the wall of separation? If handicapped children are in church-related schools, should they be refused the otherwise commonly provided state aid?

Fourth. A circuit court judge in Virginia ruled in the 1960's that there was no ground for legal action against the practice of visits by public health nurses to parochial schools. The allegation had been that tax money was thereby being used to support religious schools. Our question is whether the practice disrupts the separation principle.

A person might cite dozens of such contexts in which the problem of separation arises. The question in general is how far the State may go in aiding church-related schools and yet keep within the bounds of no-pampered or no-established church. Would it be allowable, say, on grounds of public service and secular or "general" subjects (to use Rabbi Mittlemann's word), for the State to aid in building gymnasiums for religious schools and in furnishing the best lights and seats and scientific equipment (as the National Defense Act now helps to do) and well prepared science teachers (as, indeed, the federal government is now doing with the use of National Science Foundation money)? Or is the N.S.F. procedure perhaps a case of outright disrespect for the separation principle?

All such questions are, of course, in the field of political wisdom. That is, they are very practical prudential questions, and few if any of them can be answered with a simple yes or no. Times, circumstances, needs—all such realities must be taken into consideration. Merely to say off-hand that the proposal is or is not in accord with "separation" would be like an appeal to an absolute and a dead-end, and would mean little more than empty words.

On this type of complicated problem and as a fitting conclusion to the present point, we are happy to have the legally seasoned reply of Professor Kauper. This is what he says: "At what point can it be said that financial assistance to parochial schools can be identified with religious instruction so as to make it an unconstitutional establishment? There can be no precise answer . . . the concurrence of function principle [the dual-purpose aim] is applicable here. The parochial schools do serve a recognized public purpose." If, continues Dr. Kauper, a limitation is to be observed, it is because and so far as the parochial school furthers the teaching of religion, whereas assistance for specific ends—for example, for better teaching of mathematics and science—does not.

If we might add a word to Dr. Kauper's careful statement, we would say that the teaching of mathematics and science has as its direct object and (if it is good teaching) as its direct effect the learning of mathematics. It can—the entire school or any part of it can—have extra-curricular effects that are either religious or secular, and these effects conceivably could be proscribed or effectively prohibited by an act of Congress. Nevertheless the State or the federal government, when framing a tax bill for schools or for highways, can hardly take into account all the possible religious or secular effects it may thereby accidentally promote, and it need not take them into account. It has only to look to good schools and good roads. In doing this, it sometimes does help people to go to church or to attend religiously affiliated schools. So, too, if the government were to furnish books and equipment in order that there should be good teaching of mathematics and science.

A Matter of Public Policy

It is very useful to us when legal experts such as Kauper, Katz and Sutherland make out a case for the possible constitutionality of some aid to church-related schools. Their doing so may be thought necessary because of the novel declarations of Justices Black and Rutledge in the *Everson* case, and of the former in the *McCollum* case. Yet it may be that these experts have been doing a task that is superfluous, and that all those who argue either for or against the constitutionality of such aid are engaged in love's labor lost. How so? For one thing, a case fit to try the question has never reached the Supreme Court, and quite possibly such a question could never reach it. Why not? Simply because this may turn out to be a question of public policy and not a constitutional question at all. Of course, it is in no proper sense a question of conflict between faiths.

If the federal Congress passed a law giving aid in one form or another and in one amount or another to church-related schools, it is quite possible that the question of whether the law squared with the Constitution would never and could never reach the Supreme Court. The Court might refuse the question, as it does refuse many questions. The question could be considered one of legislative policy.

Naturally this is not an issue that can be definitively resolved beforehand or on which a layman's opinion is worthy of attention. But some qualified scholars have expressed the opinion that this is a matter of legislative policy and not of fundamental law or the Constitution, and that, just as federal aid to colleges and universities is properly a matter for Congress to resolve, as indeed it does resolve it, by passing a law, so too is federal aid to schools a matter for Congress to settle one way or the other by passing or not passing a law.

Take the statements on the matter from some scholarly studies. First, in an article entitled "Public Support of Religious Education in American Constitutional Law," an article exceedingly competent from the point of view of historical study, Robert Fairfield Cushman has said that to aid or not to aid church-related education is a matter of public policy. Writing in the *Illinois Law Review* (v. 45; 1950–51, pp. 333–356), Dr. Cushman, professor of jurisprudence at Ohio State University, came (p. 349) to the following conclusion:

As the majority in the *Everson* case pointed out, a state cannot aid religion, but it can not be denied the right to aid all its children even though some of them attend religious schools. A state statute so drawn as to provide aid to all children as a group, regardless of what that aid might be, would be exceedingly difficult to attack on constitutional grounds as an aid to religion. Thus a state which provided medical service and books to all the children in the state would be virtually assured of the validity of its action.

It might be a different question, continued Dr. Cushman, if aid were designated for all children in school and some of the children were in religious schools.

Another arresting statement of the problem as one of

public policy, or, as he says, one of public good sense, is
that made by Carl N. Degler, professor of history at Vassar
College. Writing in the *Vassar Alumnae Magazine* for
February 1963, Dr. Degler remarked that it "seems very
short-sighted from a social point of view to deny assistance
to schools which educate such a large proportion of our
children." Without aid, these schools cannot do first-rate
work, and thus there must emerge from them citizens with
a less than first-rate education. "This stark fact," said Dr.
Degler, "should give all Americans pause. It raises in concrete fashion the question of whether adamant refusal to
grant some governmental support to denominational schools
is worth such a high social price. It is here not a question of
social justice but one of social intelligence."

A third study gives much the same reply: namely, that
the question is one of public policy. The late Paul M.
Butler collaborated with Alfred L. Scanlan in an article
entitled "Wall of Separation—Judicial Gloss on the First
Amendment" (*Notre Dame Lawyer*, v. 37; March, 1962,
pp. 288–308). The authors' conclusion (pp. 306–7) on the
present point is this:

> There is the opinion, and the authors share it, that if the
> Congress were to pass school aid legislation which provided
> assistance, directly or indirectly, to church-related schools,
> no one could ever successfully challenge the constitutionality
> of such a statute. It was authoritatively decided in *Massachu-
> setts v. Mellon* that an individual taxpayer, without more, does
> not have standing to bring a suit to restrain the enforcement
> of an act of Congress authorizing appropriations of public
> money upon the ground that the act is unconstitutional.

The *Mellon* decision said that a taxpayer—let us say he
was required to pay his share of taxes in support of church-
related schools—does not have "standing" to bring a suit;

he would have to demonstrate substantial diversion of funds burdening him as a taxpayer. The Supreme Court is in the habit of refusing to consider such cases. Butler and Scanlan note that their position rests on the assumption that the cited *Mellon* case (1923) was decided on constitutional grounds. They make no predictions as to whether Congress will pass any legislation in assistance of religious schools, and are careful to note modestly that "President Kennedy and the administration's spokesmen may have oversimplified or perhaps even been mistaken" in regard to what is constitutionally permissible in the form of federal aid to sectarian institutions in general.

Once a law providing aid were passed, seemingly it would hold good because it could not effectively be challenged. In an interview on this problem in 1962, Professor Arthur E. Sutherland, of Harvard University Law School, said, first, that there is no clear constitutional prohibition against federal aid to church schools, and, secondly, that if Congress passed a law providing aid, there would be no way to bring the law before the U.S. Supreme Court for a decision.

To conclude our brief treatment of aid to church schools as a matter of public policy, and also to bring together several questions already referred to, we use a summary of Dr. Kurland's article on Church and State and the Supreme Court. This summary was made by Arthur Krock in *The New York Times* (Dec. 29, 1961) under these four headings:

1. In the long series of cases asserting a breach of "the wall," the Supreme Court has never made a ruling which clearly supports the Kennedy administration's expressed legal judgment that federal aid to church-related primary

and secondary schools violates the "separation" principle;

2. The Court has had opportunities to do this, but each time has stopped short. For instance, in *Everson* it stood with parents in declaring that payments to "get their children, regardless of their religion, safely and expeditiously to and from accredited schools" were validly refunded;

3. By logical progression, this 1947 ruling would seem to put the burden on those who label as unconstitutional a federal education-aid program to finance, for all types of schools, classroom and laboratory construction;

4. Dr. Kurland's highly technical study would appear to indicate that to help or not to help private schools is an issue of public policy, and not of law.

And a Matter of Justice

Grant that aid or no aid is rather a matter of policy than of constitutionality. It is also and nevertheless a question of the justice owed by the State to citizens. This we have said, and this we will repeat. The child goes to a school chosen by his parents, and justice requires that where the child goes, his share of the educational tax dollar should go. The State has vital rights in education. But since the State does not have the primary rights in the education of children, it follows that the State does not have the sole claim to the educational tax dollar.

A cut in that dollar belongs, in distributive justice, to those—namely, the parents—who have the primary right and responsibility for the education of the child.

Many distinguished scholars and statesmen are beginning to say what we have just said. Roger A. Freeman, of Claremont College, says: "There is an injustice in our method of restricting State and local school support to one school system of a quasi-monopoly character." William W. Brickman says it is "decidedly unjust," Wilber Katz says it is an "unjust burden," and Senator Keating of New York says "there is injustice."

6 · Pluralism in American Education

The Pluralist Fact and Problem

In our country, schools and education have experienced and thrived on a great heterogeneity. At first and for a long time the majority of schools and colleges were non-state and non-public. People who wanted either schools or colleges (levels were not well marked) set them up and somehow maintained them. The people in question were for the most part churchmen and concerned believers, and as a result most of our early educational institutions were not only independent but church-related.

On the lower levels, our schools were commonly founded by Protestants, and many of them were state-financed and thus represented a union of Church, State and school. On the higher levels, even today the independent colleges and universities, often church-related, outnumber the state-related ones. Over the past one hundred years we have also established more and more state colleges and universities, and for financial rather than academic reasons the total number of students in these is growing faster than that in the independent colleges and universities. The private-public diversity thus has been and is one of the commonest characteristics of American education.

Besides, we inevitably have various levels of education which automatically add a minor note of diversity. But the major note comes from the continuing fact of public schools and independent schools on all levels. Among the chief differences between these two, as we said, is that the former is entirely or almost entirely supported by tax money, and the independent schools receive relatively little tax money and many of them receive from the public till no direct subvention at all. By indirection and yet effectively, the independent schools do benefit from official state accommodation, since, as we have remarked, like public schools and like all non-profit and beneficent institutions they are exempt from paying property taxes.

Many schools of many types and several levels—that is the given situation. Yet all, whatever the type or the level, are called to work together. This is a point on which, as citizens and educators, we must insist, and it is the main point of the present and the succeeding chapter. All schools —each severally and all together—are called to serve the good of the child and therefore the good of the citizen and also concurrently to serve the public or common good. Serving the child and the nation is the school's vocation, and among us this should automatically be a pluralistic service.

Here we have at once the pluralistic fact in education and the pluralistic problem and implied law in education. The *fact* is a vast variety of types and levels. That is the given situation with which educators are always confronted, and we will say and repeat that the genuine educational statesman, whether his reach is nation-wide or only state-wide, must take that situation into account; to be a full fledged American educator, he must never fight shy of high or low schools, private or public schools. The *problem* is how all can work together for the common national educational good as well as for the good of the youths of all ages, committed to them for the time being. The *law* is that educators should so work; they are to work together and for the common national educational good.

All this is simple on paper—every school, every level and every type at work in its own bailiwick, each encouraged and enabled to work with a notable freedom, and yet each learning how to work with all toward the common educational good. But in practice, it has certainly proved to be difficult, and in this chapter we must emphasize that, though it is certainly done, it is far from being fully or even satisfactorily done, and that most teachers and perhaps many superintendents of private as well as of public schools are unaware that this pluralistic working is an essential part of their job. This failure to accept the theory and practice of pluralism is one of the greatest weaknesses in American education, and educators scarcely notice the failure and are offended when one mentions it. In the following discussion we want to name and to underline ways in which educators can begin to achieve the naturally required pluralism.

Simple as the pluralistic fact or situation is, and simple and obvious as are the problem and the law of pluralism, we must nevertheless carefully state the general meaning of "pluralism." We repeat that it might seem odd that this needs to be done. One would scarcely believe how innocent of the fact and problem and law are many of our written "philosophies of education." Of the first dozen of them I examined in this connection, the lack of awareness was impressive. A volume by Dr. Ulich, of Harvard, had a good brief treatment of pluralism in education, and a volume by Dr. Phenix, of Columbia, had useful remarks on the general and the particular situation; another author quoted one sentence from Maritain on pluralism, and an inferior volume had a chapter on unity and diversity, which is exactly the question. It is incredible that seven of the twelve said not a single word on pluralism, though among the titles were these: *Foundations for a Philosophy of Education* (1961); *Organic Philosophy of Education* (1957); *A Living Philosophy of Education* (1940); and *Democratic Educational Theory* (1960).

The Meaning of Pluralism

All the more need, therefore, to make clear what we mean in general by "pluralism," and how educational theory and practice are required to fit into the pluralist picture, especially in the United States.

This is the description of pluralism given by Webster: "1: the quality or state of being plural . . . 4a: a state or condition of society in which members of diverse ethnic, racial, religious, or social groups maintain an autonomous participation in and development of their traditional culture within the confines of a common civilization) b: a concept, doctrine, or policy proposing or advocating this state." *both freedom of groups & for common good.*

Webster's "4a" presupposes his "1," and, as we are not proposing or advocating "a state or condition" but accepting and describing it, we may proceed with the fact or situation—the "state or condition"—of society in which each of various groups, such as Jews or Catholics or Protestants or secularists, has its own philosophy and theology, its own way of seeing man and the world, and its consequent pattern of conduct, and yet (we hope) does, consciously and/or unconsciously, work with the other groups to build one common good and one common civilization. Each group is free to have its own theory of man and his place in nature, and this theory may only more or less coincide with the theories of the other groups. At the same time, each group must be presumed to have the wisdom and the good will to work with the other groups at the common national task. There is a common national work to be done by each working freely and independently, if it chooses, and by all freely working together.

Next, we cite several scholars who have summed up what they take to be the best way to state the meaning of "pluralism." Political philosopher and historian Eric Voegelin points out that in today's democratic societies, we have to do with many diverse groups; for instance, with Catholics and Protestants, with old-style liberals and "plain secular liberals," and so on. "This rich diversification of socially entrenched and violently vociferous opinion is what we call our pluralistic society." Voegelin says that the reality is far from a genteel picture of men peacefully searching for truth; in everyday life, we have groups with radically different views.

Theologian John Courtney Murray says that a freely pluralistic organization of the community is to be expected since many different answers are actually given by various groups to the ultimate questions, such as: What is man? Is man wholly of a piece with nature? What is man's highest good, and where is it attainable? Widely differing replies to questions in mathematics or physics might conceivably cause little concern, but differing replies to the most basic human problems must be a basic human concern; and yet of course in making replies to human problems, men and groups should be left free. Says Father Murray: "All these questions, and others related to them, concern the essentials of human existence. The multiplicity of answers to them is in general what we mean by modern pluralism." Here the reference is only to the pluralistic fact, and not to any doctrine or policy defending or advocating the fact.

The next statement is by another man of distinction, a statement eulogizing what the author sees as pluralism in our country. In *Cultural Pluralism and the American Idea*, social theorist Horace Kallen has said: "This process is an orchestration of diverse utterances of diversities—regional, local, religious, esthetic, industrial, sporting and political— each developing freely and characteristically in its own enclave, and somehow so intertwined with the others as to suggest, even to symbolize, the dynamic of the whole. Each is a cultural reservoir whence flows its own singularity of expression to unite in the concrete intercultural total which is the culture of America."

Dr. Kallen's next observation, made in regard to the "inter" in intercultural, goes to the core. The "inter," he says, postulates the parity of the different elements and "their free and friendly communication with one another as both co-operators and competitors."

Let us sharpen the several statements to read: on the one hand, we have groups with their own several traditions, each with its own philosophy and theology, and perfectly free, so far as public policy and practice are concerned, to live by its own traditions and philosophy and theology. That is one side of the picture. The other side is that each group has to work for the common good, and is not morally free not to work for the common good, along with groups that may have traditions and habits and philosophies and theologies notably different from its own.

On the one hand we have the freedom of groups, on the other hand the moral commitment of each group and all groups to work for the common good. Each group must be allowed to be free—this is a "must" and allows no freedom. And each group must work with each other group and with all groups for the common good—this, too, is a "must" and allows no freedom, or at any rate only that higher freedom which consists of working with all for the common good. The persisting problem is to respect all proper and non-heretical diversity while achieving a defensible unity. But why should one add "non-heretical"? Because to attempt to go with a communist group aiming to destroy our freedom and even our existence, could not make sense. Hence the importance of the operative ideas "orthodoxy" and "heresy."

The old, old problem of which we are speaking, then, is the problem of the one and the many, of unity and diversity, and this in relation to social and not immediately to metaphysical problems. Before we proceed to mention the incidence of the problem in the cosmos and in general human affairs, we want to illustrate and underline its significance in America. In terms of traditions and basic philosophies and theologies and faiths, the chief groups among us are Jews, Catholics, Protestants and secularists, each of them rather well-marked, though the first and the last tend to overlap. We have said that the pluralist fact is a two-sided situation, a one-in-many or a many-in-one situation. Jews see and believe differently from either Catholics or Protestants. As a group they see ABC to be the proper understanding of a situation. But in the same context, Catholics might see ABD to be the proper understanding and Protestants might see it as ABE. It has happened and will happen again that one group, in one way or another, pressures another group to see eye to eye with it, above all in relation to public policy and practice; for example, on birth control devices or absolute separation or evolution or on the use of alcohol. The group may, of course, use persuasion and propaganda to try to convert other groups to its way of understanding and justifying, and in the private life of its own members it may practice as it sees fit, as long as its practice does not interfere with the freedom and rights of others.

The freedom side, however, is only one side, and has to be kept balanced against the public-good side. Jews, for instance, may freely understand as Jews and believe as Jews. They may also in many matters be well justified in working for Jews, but they would rarely be justified in anything like countering or at all neglecting the good of the whole people. Jews are too important a segment in our nation for them to ghettoize themselves in seeking good. So too of secularists and Catholics and Protestants. There was a day in our history when it might conceivably have been allowable for Protestants to go simply for the good of Protestants, but that day is long past. We live in a pluralist society, and the practice, common to this day, of Protestants or Catholics or Jews seeking their own good almost exclusively must be condemned and transcended.

I am thinking here of words or actions or policies by responsible leaders or groups, and of words or actions or policies that have considerable social effect; trivial words or actions may be disregarded in the present context. We concede that sometimes a group, being deprived of a good coming to it, could be justified in using fair means to preserve and promote its own good even though a resultant side issue would be that the general public good would for a time suffer. Instances of such goods coming to a group would be the right of Negroes or others to have employment and housing, to vote, hold office and enjoy a cut in the tax dollar. These goods it may on occasion seek in spite of some immediate loss to the general good; to deny its right to do so would mean that it must continue to suffer injustice.

In passing we reply to an objection occasionally heard. Why not let bad enough alone? Why not let sleeping dogs lie? Are not the religious faiths well treated in America? Where has religion ever been freer? Given such a favorable climate, why not honor the pluralist principle by saying nothing? Why stir up a hornets' nest by suggesting any aid at all for church-related schools? To do so would increase tension and conflict!

The implied argument is that peoples and faiths have suffered more injustice in other times and places, and therefore those now wanting freedoms and a fair deal should desist and should be glad to suffer.

Now to return to the very meaning of the pluralistic situation. We have expressed it by saying that Jews, for example, are to be free to go their own way with their own beliefs and philosophies as far as their doing so is attuned to the general social good, or at least is not against that good. And likewise for Catholics and Protestants and secularists. Let us express this in another way. Neither in theory nor practice will men ever over-emphasize either the freedom side or the common good side as long as they duly respect the other side. This "rich diversification of socially entrenched and violently vociferous opinion," as Voegelin has formulated it, is one side. The other side is what Maritain says amounts to affirming "the same set of convictions concerning action" for the public good. The former side is allowed and encouraged, the latter is ethically required. The freedom side is good, and the common good side is good, but only on condition that each in its turn is circumspect and allows generously for the other. Just how much freedom to allow to a group cannot be said on paper, or just how much to expect it to bend its interests and freedoms to the common good. It depends on circumstances, such as peace and war and other crises, and also on the maturity of a people; and the circumstances are always changing. The decision must be left to the wise prudential judgment of voters and above all to the decision of rulers. It would be impossible to make out a once-for-all map to cover the matter.

In Nature and the Cosmos

So much just now for the relevance of the pluralistic idea to the social life of the nation, and the idea as seen to be based on well-known social facts. The social situation is plural, of course, since it is many-stranded and made up of many things of many kinds; it is pluralistic in the dual sense already emphasized. A pluralist society, however, has nothing essentially to do with the Church-State question or with "establishment" or "disestablishment"; France without an established church is a pluralist society, and so is England, with an established church.

Moreover, the one and the many run through nature as well as through human affairs and are basic to the whole of nature. The living plant or animal is one and yet is compounded of many constituents working together for a common end; and a rock or a planet, or again the entire given interrelated natural world, has its many elements making an ordered totality. The social order made by man and demanded by nature is plural, and should, at least in a heterogeneous society, be pluralistic; and the natural order found by man is plural and at least has all the look of being pluralistic, each part of it having a kind of spontaneity and autonomy and yet being subordinated to the total order. That is the way of nature and also of the good society, whether in the family, the school, the economy, the Church or the State, or in the ensemble of these and other factors making up the "body politic."

Pluralism in Aristotle

Aristotle never used the word *pluralism* but was well acquainted with the idea and the reality. He said that the good society will always be pluralistic, and he found radical fault with the doctrine of Socrates expressed by Plato that the military class should not be free to have their own wives and their own property, but should have wives and property in common.

The evil seen so clearly by Socrates and Plato was granted by Aristotle to be real and serious. It was conflict, disruption, disunity in society; and the good sought, namely the guaranteeing of social unity, was likewise granted to be a basic good. The Socratic-Platonic principle was also seen to be commendable; it was that society should have unity. But too much was asked of this principle, and in this case the desired unity would have to be purchased at too high a price. One side of the pluralistic picture, the social harmony side, would have all the care lavished on it, and the other side, that of free persons and free associations, would be disrespected. The ideal result of the freedom of the many combined with the unity of all would be lost.

Balancing the two sides was for Aristotle an important consideration. For him, this balancing meant saving a fundamental principle by honoring it, and concurrently saving its complementary principle. Even so, Aristotle thought it was a question of saving more than a principle, for he thought the issue at bottom was the saving or the destroying of the State. He said that the very life of the State consists in balancing the one and the many: freedoms of the many always allowed and encouraged, but always kept in subordination to an overriding national good. Unity in plurality, and plurality in unity—otherwise the State itself is destroyed.

Obviously, this balancing and harmonizing the freedoms of the many with the overriding national good and unity is a perpetual problem, and, as remarked above, it cannot be handled in a blueprint or map. Nevertheless, it is done and has always been done, and the problem is not novel or peculiar to our age. Hitler could not do it, and neither could any ancient or modern totalitarian dictator. Such a man refuses to honor the freedom side, and all think at once of the unfortunate persons and groups who accordingly lose their freedom. At the same time, Aristotle said that such theorists and practitioners, from Socrates to communist leaders, are doing something worse than negating the freedoms of persons and groups. He said that they are really destroying the State, because "the good of things must be that which preserves them." This was Aristotle's basic principle in the matter, a principle grasped in its full implications when it is expressed in the double negative: "That which is destructive of things cannot be the good of things." That which destroys the State cannot be the good of the State.

Is the pluralistic problem, in education or the economy or in family life, as serious as all that? Is the free association side, the free belief side—for example, of Jews or Catholics

—so radical and serious? Aristotle certainly thought so, and we have reason to think so. The crushing of freedoms, to hold office, to work, to vote, to operate and patronize schools, is hard on the victims, but it could also eventually mean the destruction of the State, the genius of which consists in balancing the freedom side with the unity and common good side. On the one hand, we may not let our freedoms run wild, but must keep them attuned first and last to the public good; and on the other, we may not let national or any other unity destroy the freedom of men and groups. Aristotle thought that doing this latter would be hard not merely on the immediate victims, such as the Negro today in the Deep South, but would be against the nature and being of the State; and he meant any good state, and not only a good democratic state.

Here is Aristotle's conclusion: "Hence it is evident that a state is not by nature one in that sense which some persons affirm; and that what is said to be the greatest good of cities is in reality their destruction."[1] Evidently, then, Aristotle took a dim view of the non-pluralistic and monistic and monolithic State or society. The nature of the State is to be made up of many persons and groups freely working together for the common good; and to minimize either the freedom of the many or the end—namely, the common good—must be to do injury, not only to the good of man, but to the whole social order required by nature.

There are popular ways to say what Aristotle said. For instance, "to overdo anything is to spoil it." "Too much of a good thing is as bad as too little" and "Don't work a willing horse to death." Let us try putting "pluralism" in capsule form and in axioms. Then it would read: "The common good and national unity, yes; the destruction of

[1] Aristotle's *Politics*, Book II, cc. 1–2.

freedoms, no. The promotion of freedoms, yes; the destruction of the common good and national unity, no."

In any case, all can see how relevant are Aristotle's principles in the matter, and how basic pluralism is to his philosophy of society.

Aristotle states the freedom principle as a matter of fact; that is, he assumes it. On this principle, St. Thomas Aquinas is at once more radical than Aristotle and has a more fundamental respect for man's freedoms. He has more respect for freedom, because he says that "man is not subordinate in all that he is and all that he has to any political community." He is more radical because he says that man is indeed thus subordinate to God; he grants that man is in many ways subordinated to man and to the political community, but certainly not in a total way. Of course, Aquinas is speaking of what is right and just by nature or natural law, and not of what may actually be done under some Hitler or Castro.

Pluralism in Secondary Areas

From what is said of pluralism by various scholars, we might sometimes suppose that unless a people had diversity in philosophies and theologies, its social life would be without pluralism; and the supposition actually has some warrant. This is the case because the main human diversities are in philosophies and theologies, and to some extent these diversities are sure to occur. But as a consequence of diversity in basic philosophies and theologies, and also by chance, diversity can also occur in secondary areas of vast importance, such as the political, the educational, and the economic. Consider merely the last named. In our own country we have a mixed economy which is at once individual, familial, cooperative, state, and corporation. All these make one over-all economy, each is at least allowed or perhaps even encouraged to go its own way with its own techniques, and all ideally (and, as a rule, actually) work together toward the common economic good. Each has autonomy, though within some sort of common good limits and restraints. None of them may simply shoulder the others out. The economy, local, regional and national, is thus an instance, in a wide and yet restricted field, of several diverse groups, each with freedom, and all making a unity. Here as elsewhere the effective and harmonious working together of the one and the many, with freedom allowed to each, inevitably creates problems that cannot be solved in an advance way and once for all.

As just remarked, diversity in any of the four areas mentioned may arise in part from more basic philosophical or theological diversities. For example, the gap between Birchites and liberals may be something far deeper than politics and economics; and again as far as there is conflict between public and private education, the gap is almost certain to rest on something more basic than disagreement on textbooks or how to spend the tax dollar.

American Education Is Pluralistic

Now that we have cleared the way on the meaning of "pluralism," it is easiest to begin with the obvious fact that the educational life in America, whatever its quality, is pluralistic. Everybody sees that what are called the two educational systems, public and private, are concurrently existing and operating. It is a slight and pardonable exaggeration to say that as long as we have had any formal education in this country, the two have been concurrent.

The private, church-related was first on the scene; but without notable injustice to either, we may say that the two are simply coeval. For generations, the two were existing together, they now are and they will be existing together. How long will this coexistence continue? We may suppose as long as the nation. We have not the slightest reason to think that the public or private schools will disappear, though perhaps one will increase faster than the other and even at the expense of the other. The two overlap at some points now, and we shall argue that, for the good of each and for the over-all national educational good, they should do far more than overlap. Yet no doubt the two will continue, each with freedom and with a relative independence, and with many of its own procedures.

The given situation is the pluralistic character of our educational life. That is the way our educational life has been and the way it presumably will always be. It is dual; and surely, on any ideal view or any defensible view, it is one. A corollary is that any educational policy that neglects or slights one or the other type of school, the public or the private, is unrealistic and unworkable, and is outside the American ideal and should be outside the American educational scene.

Each Type Indispensable

In some out-of-the-way places, some village or rural school district, we could and do get along without one type or the other, and there the schools can advisedly be all public or all private. They cannot—in practice or on American principles—be all public or all private in Chicago or New York or Boston or San Francisco or in any city; and since the bulk of our population is progressively locating in cities and suburbs, it should be clear to all that, even if we wanted to, we could not now get along without either the public or the private schools.

The United States Office of Education reported "about 480,000 pupils on curtailed sessions in 1962 in 37 states and the District of Columbia. Only 10 states reported that they had no children on shortened sessions. . . . About two-thirds of the children who were receiving less than a full day's education were on the elementary level, with the remaining one-third in high school. . . . The reported shortage of classrooms in the fall of 1962 was 121,200." Naturally if the some seven millions attending private elementary and high schools were thrown on the generally overcrowded public schools, there would be a greatly aggravated shortage of space and manpower, and at least the physical indispensability of the private schools would be evident.

Our statement about indispensability holds for schools on any and every level, primary, secondary and college; but since in this connection most persons think of the lower levels, we are willing to make our assertion merely of them. For instance, the private and parochial primary schools in Chicago and its suburbs are indispensable. Chicago and its suburbs could not live and breathe educationally without them. Perhaps someone will argue that it is a bad thing to have these private parochial schools; perhaps they are divisive, and perhaps to be divisive is always and manifestly a bad thing. We waive these issues at the moment. If the Catholic parochial primary schools in Chicago or any large city were to close, the city would be in trouble, which means that the children, the parents, the schools and the taxpayers would all be in trouble. When in the spring of 1963, students from several parochial schools erupted on public schools in several Missouri towns and cities, some of those public schools were so incommoded that they had to close. At least in that sense, of finance and housing and manpower, the city and its citizens must recognize the private schools as well as the public schools as indispensable.

But all of us will have to recognize each type as indispensable in a deeper and far more significant sense. Each is indispensable to the idea of education in America. That idea is essentially pluralistic, and when, according to Theodore Powell's report, a Rhode Island man said his church council wanted all children to have a "truly American education in the one public elementary school system," the man and his council were appealing to a monolithic and un-American principle quite at variance with reality. So, too, was the American Federation of Teachers in its 1947 declaration: "The basic principle that the interests of the democratic society are best served where children of all component groups of American society are enrolled in a common public school." Actually, the Federation's appeal was to a principle basic to the monolithic and dictator society. So also of the almost dictatorial statement made in 1963 by Professor L. Harold DeWolf, of Boston University School of Theology: "Every aristocratic, class-conscious private elementary school and every religious, parochial school is an enemy of the community and of our free institutions." That was a formula that one might expect from Hitler, Stalin or Mussolini.

Why make so strong a statement? Because at the heart of the American and democratic idea, in education and all social institutions, is freedom, and therefore—as Aristotle would insist—pluralism. Not only to destroy freedoms, but to constrain them and make life hard for them, is contrary to our traditions and practices and to the American idea.

Therefore to pressure the private or the public primary schools and in effect "to put the squeeze on" them would be at least as un-American as to pressure and try to destroy family ownership or individual or cooperative or corporation ownership, and would be as bad as to pressure the freedom of the press. Our life is democratic and pluralistic, and to wipe out this basic mark of it would be to give us something communist or fascist—anything but American. Our people have wanted private and public schools on all levels; they have organized them and continue to want them and to have them. This is a phenomenon within the general and national freedom and democratic phenomenon, and precisely within the American idea. Freedom to make a choice in type of school is something as indispensable—because indispensable to the American idea—as, for instance, freedom to vote or to worship as one pleases.

The pluralistic way in education is the only way our schools exist. That is precisely what Justice McReynolds said in writing the unanimous decision in favor of freedom in the *Oregon* case (1925) (He said that other nations, with other views of reality and of man—"philosophies," he called them—have required all to attend one monolithic type of school, but our people, thinking and operating freely and pluralistically, have, he went on to declare, encouraged freedom in types of schools and education. This point of parents' rights having the priority was in effect repeated in the Supreme Court decision in *Prince v. Massachusetts* (1944): "It is cardinal with us that the custody, care, and nurture of the child reside first in the parents, whose primary function and freedom include preparation for obligations the State can neither supply nor hinder."

Our point at the moment is that if one type of school were made to suffer, or if the primary rights of the parents in education were made to yield to the real though secondary rights of the State, the American idea of freedom would be made to suffer. All grant that the rights of the State are important, but the rights of parents are yet more basic, and because each type of school is indispensable in both the practical and the ideal order, we are morally bound to encourage both. To do otherwise would be both un-American and unethical.

The American people want a real and considerable freedom for each type, and we who write these words want a genuine and far more conscious working together of the types than is actually in evidence today. This working together is the other indispensable half of the pluralistic way in education.

Remarking in his *Philosophy of Education* that "we live today, especially in this country, in a 'pluralistic' society with many layers of opinion," Professor Robert Ulich, of Harvard, has pointed out that among us no one philosophy may expect sovereignty in education; not, he said, a Christian orthodoxy, nor a utilitarian cast of mind, nor "the tyranny of science," nor again what he called a dogmatic educational pragmatism and experimentalism. What he was saying was that we might as well get things straight; namely, that we have varying basic general philosophies of man and nature and these philosophies go over consistently into varying philosophies of education, of which we also have many. Consequently, to attempt to make American education monolithic by declaring that this or that is *the* American philosophy of education is to be dogmatic and somewhat naïve. So, too, regarding any attempt to force a monolithic system of education on a free people.

Since we have this freedom to hold various philosophies of education, as American citizens we also have freedom to operate and promote corresponding and consequent types of education.

The Problem of Cooperating

This fact of many philosophies of education is a second major pluralistic fact on the American educational horizon; and this fact, along with public and private schools, is enough to establish the pluralistic character of American educational enterprise. But we must come at once to the other side of the pluralistic educational picture. There are various philosophies and there are the two basic types of schools. The other side of the picture is that *the two types must find ways of working together,* and so must the proponents of all philosophies. We shall proceed therefore to emphasize the obligation that the leaders in the two types lie under to learn how to work together. Today they are far apart and are making few if any efforts to achieve unity, and, as we remarked, are unaware of the problem. Private and public educators must learn to work together and, in doing so, to advance rather than to destroy freedom.

Speaking of leaders in the two types of education, public and private, let us as an initial step classify the several ways in which these leaders ordinarily do or do not now cooperate. The schools and their leaders tend to work today in any of the four following manners.

First of all, the two types or their leaders may be more or less mutually exclusive; that is often the actual condition, each type of school, public and private, going its own individualistic way with hardly a thought that the two types are supposedly achieving an effectively united national school front. This mutually exclusive way holds at both the local and the national level, and above all in the primary and secondary schools. The local primary parochial schools—for instance, Catholic, some Christian Reformed (as in central Michigan), some Lutheran, the three hardly aware even of each other—are likely to bother their heads little if at all about the problems and the welfare of the local public schools, and most likely the public schools perpetually return the compliment. It is as if each of the two types had a perfect right to develop in isolation, and could do so. The result is that the two are poles apart. The same is true nationally; officials in HEW (which stands for Heath, Education and Welfare), an office with federal cabinet rank, have consistently been dodging, as far as possible, the problems of the private primary schools, and these important officials are embarrassed when they have to consider those problems, the embarrassment arising from political and not from educational concerns. HEW has at times thought and acted for the sake of secondary private schools, but evidently it would prefer to avoid any and all issues connected with schools below college. The reason, of course, is that, in the popular and vote-conferring mind, there is supposed to be some kind of mystic constitutional gap between a college freshman and a high school senior.

Here is an instance on both the state and federal level of the education department ignoring the lower private schools. In 1963, the Education Department of New York State, with a grant of $82,500 from the United States Office of Education, launched what should develop into a significant program of integrating the arts—music, the visual arts and theater arts—into high school curricula. The experiment was begun in six public high schools. Our only suggested criticisms would be two; first, that, with the state full of private high schools, the limitation to public schools means that the experiment misses its fullest educational opportunity, and, secondly, that the Education Department of New York, afraid of or unaware of the pluralist problem and law of education in America, is an inadequate and half-hearted state educational department.

In general, in this unfortunate theory and practice, there is a marked tendency locally, nationally and state-wide to keep public schools in one airtight compartment and private schools in another. This we shall call the policy and practice of mutual exclusion, and it amounts to a tacit denial of educational pluralism and of our actual local and national condition. Leaders in each type of school act as if the other type did not exist. This cannot be good for either type or for general progress in education.

A second way, and certainly not a better one, is to generate tensions, oppositions and conflicts which are likely to be mutual and may occur for either ideological or practical reasons, though most often they occur only on account of ignorance and hold-over bad habits. For example, some persons patronizing parochial schools may become unhappy and restive about paying taxes to public schools, and there no doubt are instances in which some join other restive citizens to vote against increased taxes for really needed public school improvement; and this sort of balking at educational improvement can happen on either the local or the national scene. Some also are unfriendly to public schools for religious reasons, even going as far as to say that these schools are godless.

On occasion, churchmen become virulent against public schools, and the irony of it is that some of these churchmen may perhaps never have been inside a public school. In this regard, some public school officials may be quite uninformed, too, and may know far too little of what goes on in the neighboring private school: neither the churchmen nor the public school officials know what the other type of school does, what it needs, what are its rights and values.

These two unworthy and as if opposed attitudes have been well suggested by Theodore Powell, Public Information Consultant of the Connecticut State Department of Education. Mr. Powell, well qualified to speak, has said that non-Catholics "rarely have reason or opportunity to go inside the Catholic school," and, on the other hand, "the attitude of public school administrators frequently has been less than hospitable."[2]

Sometimes, too, the great national associations act as if their chief function was to make life difficult for private schools. An incredible instance of this occurred when, in 1962, Dr. Carr, then president of the National Educational Association, sent telegrams to national legislators urging them not to take a step that might be calculated to help private schools. His action was blind and narrow, since he was then the highest official in a supposedly significant and responsible national educational organization and since we might presume that he himself was an educator and a responsible citizen. He evidenced no grasp at all of the pluralism that education in America is bound to allow for and to express. Likewise, the resolutions frequently passed against private schools by national education associations do little credit to the breadth of vision of the officers and members.

It is an unfortunate moment for education and the national good when schools, now public, now private, are thus unfairly dealt with and when either tax payers or churchmen or men sitting in the place of educators resort

[2] Theodore Powell. *Bulletin*, National Catholic Educational Association, 58 (1961), pp. 210–211.

to politics and subterfuge, and can do no better than oppose, blast and counterblast. All such attitudes and practices may be summed up as the policy and practice of opposition and conflict, and, whereas some tension is to be expected and accepted, the way of opposition and conflict is almost sure to be a bad one. We must believe that, with good will and a little effort, free and intelligent men could do something better than this.

The third way, that of tolerance, is notably better, though by itself, of course, it is insufficient. We are living in a highly pluralistic society, and this requires the working together in unity of divers and sometimes diverse groups, a working for the general national good. Pluralism in education has to mean exactly that kind of unified working, and therefore a mere tolerance of public and private schools for each other, a policy of live and let live, is inadequate. This is true in education and in every important social area. *The New York Times* reports: "The pace of desegregation is not satisfactory to many Negro leaders. But there can be no question that some progress is being made, in understanding, tolerance, acceptance and good will." This is much; and yet, after all, toleration is far from enough. In education or in race relations, it is evident that a mutual bearing with one another is required. But this is scarcely a minimum first step. Good as it is, toleration is not nearly good enough, and in the present matter, as in other human concerns, a mere toleration is a kind of insult. Suppose a boy merely tolerates his father, or a man merely tolerates his wife. Is the situation really much better when Catholics and Protestants merely tolerate each other, or Christians merely tolerate Jews, or private and public educators merely tolerate each other? Is it ever enough when people merely put up with people? We are morally bound to seek to achieve mutual esteem and mutual charity, both in theory and practice.

Look at "mere tolerance" from another point of view. Is the situation of bare tolerance a great deal better than for the two types of schools to disregard each other? In either case, the two lie fallow alongside each other, with never a creative thought or act, each of them almost as good as dead as far as the other's good or the total good is concerned. The policy and the practice of tolerance are a far cry from a living and organic educational system and from achieving a democratic pluralism in which "the one" would be made up of the harmonious working together of "the many," and yet each of the many would enjoy its own autonomy.

7 · The Ideal and Blessed Condition

The Fourth Attitude

We come, therefore, to a statement of the fourth attitude, which would be the ideal and blessed condition. This would be the cooperation of the many for the common good, and this cooperative pluralism would be as important in education as in any part of our national life. Here as elsewhere, the partisan for only his own purposes and his own group is less than half good enough.

The idea of *e pluribus unum* must become effective and operative in education. However, this is much easier said than done. An actual cooperating of the basic types in education ought to be relatively easy; but it is going to take much more thought and effort than the best of our educators have yet given to it. We have already noted how nescient even our philosophers are on the problem and law of pluralism; and we may be sure that our practice is not better than our theory. Because pluralistic educational cooperation is so basic and at the same time so much neglected, it is high time for somebody to emphasize it.

As a first step in thinking about cooperation, let us cite the well-advised position of Professor Philip H. Phenix, of Columbia University, in his *Philosophy of Education*. Dr. Phenix says (pp. 519–521) that any educator willing to see realities is automatically committed to pluralism: goals in education are many, situations are different, any two men are different, many and varied truths are given, and in various situations we have to invoke a multiplicity of rules; and since we must see that there are many ways of believing and doing, the resulting minimum demanded of the educator is "tolerance and generosity toward those who differ" from him. Everywhere, says Dr. Phenix (pp. 82, 219, 224–5), we encounter the fact of plurality, a plurality of religions, of scientific inquiry, of patterns of livelihood, and many diversified groups in a society at once diversified and unified; and since we believe in rights for persons and groups, one of our chief duties must always be "encouraging diversity within unity."

Dr. Phenix and Dr. Ulich, and every philosopher and educator at all alerted to social realities, would say that a major problem in educational policy and practice in America has to be the problem of coming to terms with the naturally imposed problem of pluralism. The pluralistic fact is only the beginning of the problem. We have to learn to make room perpetually for the working out of diversities, first of all in freedom, and concurrently and always toward the common educational good. To balk at either side, the free and diversified side or the common-social-good side, is to be at best only half an educator.

That is not yet the whole story. Each side working in freedom, and each working for the total common good—this is not yet enough. The two must learn to work together.

Who in particular is to do this cooperating? We do not suggest that every parent or every primary teacher should see and labor to promote the two sides of pluralism or their working together. But every leading educator and every philosopher of education should see them and work to promote a pluralistic result. If a man does not do this, we would have to say he is scarcely an educator at all, and certainly not a philosopher of education. The two sides and their working together should also be seen and promoted by everyone—for example, journalist, statesman, churchman—who has any considerable influence on educational practice. At both the local and the national level, policy and practice should be shaped by the cooperating of the two sides for the general educational good.

From a financial point of view, it has been found that a particular state does well to work pluralistically by furnishing aid to private education. At least, this is the experience of those states which now assist education at private colleges: they say they could not afford not to furnish aid. The official California *Statement on State Scholarships* says: "The Legislature recognized that the cost of tuitional scholarships to independent colleges represented less than the cost of educating a student at a public university, and that there was a resultant saving to the taxpayer." The State Scholarship Plan, allowing students in California to choose public or private colleges, "has resulted in substantial savings to the taxpayers in terms of capital investments, structural facilities, and operating costs." The pluralistic character of such aiding has also been well stated by the Regents of New York State: "The variety of sponsorship and support reflects the pluralism of our country." Other states are proceeding on somewhat similar principles, for instance, Illinois, Maryland, Massachusetts, Missouri, New Jersey and Rhode Island.

The two values which recommend this procedure on the college level should recommend it on the lower levels. The values are a saving to the taxpayer—in "capital investments, structural facilities, and operating costs"—and the pluralistic and American way.

Demanding freedoms for types of schools, for styles of teaching, and for modes of inquiry and selection of materials, allowing freedoms of thought and philosophies and beliefs and theologies—all of this goes with one necessary component of pluralism and democracy in education. The other component, also absolutely required, is the working together of all educators and types of schools for the good of every child and the general social good.

Of course, many things such as libraries and other equipment are to be made to serve their parts in effecting the values just now mentioned. But naturally it is persons such as teachers and administrators and educational leaders and philosophers and the several associations and the ideological groups which are, so far as reasonably possible, to be united in achieving the over-all educational good.

For Whom This Liberty?

At least in the democratic society, it is axiomatic that no person or group is to be penalized for exercising normal and constitutional freedoms. As previously stated, the Oregon or *Pierce* decision of 1925 made what one might think as somehow superfluous the official declaration that persons or groups may establish and operate private schools. But if they are to be penalized in the exercise of this freedom, it is a dubious asset to them, somewhat akin to the freedom a man has to climb a wall though he is horse-whipped every time he reaches the top. The case is like that of a child who is allowed to go out to swim, but is not allowed to go near the water. In such circumstances, it would appear to be a misfortune to be free. There is a perverseness and sadism in saying that groups of parents are free to patronize schools of their choice, in order, as they affirm, to exercise constitutionally guaranteed religious freedom for themselves and their children, and at the same time saying that if they want these schools they must pay both for them and for public schools which they may not feel free in conscience to use. The freedom is only alleged and is at best theoretic; the free exercise of religion, guaranteed by the First Amendment, is made to suffer.

The freedom to exercise a freedom which, at least for poorer families, is next to impossible, looks like a cruel one, and its beneficiaries might say: "O terrible freedom, with a double-tax clause attached and a price tag on it!" It will not do for a poor man to have a conscience in regard to where and how and by whom his children shall be educated.

That is just what some competent observers have said of this freedom. In an article called "The Freedom to Believe," Professor Wilber Katz, then of Chicago University Law School and now of Wisconsin, said in the *Atlantic Monthly* in 1953: "We exact a price for the exercise of this liberty." Perhaps it is eminently fair to do so, but this is a point that would have to be considered in any honest attempt to honor the First Amendment in its non-interference clause, to achieve justice and work out a pluralistic national educational policy. The *Pierce* decision, unanimously in favor of those wanting private schools, said that the parents or guardians who nurture the child and direct his destiny "have the right, coupled with the high duty, to recognize and prepare him for additional obligations" besides those imposed by the State, and that among those rights and freedoms was that to send him to schools of their choice.

The question, however, is precisely whether in the concrete this right and freedom of choice amounts to anything more than empty assertion. For the wealthy, it certainly can amount to more; they can afford freedom of choice. But if this freedom of choice and of religious education is limited to the wealthy, then the relevant legislating and judging appear like discrimination against poor people and ordinary families. Perhaps the court, in announcing the freedom, should have added a footnote that this freedom is mostly for the rich.

Let us repeat this neglected point. Both the wealthy and the poor are declared to have this right to choose education for their children, but only the wealthy can afford to have it, and therefore the legislating and the Court's judging seem to be weighted against the poor. The result is that the freedom of the poor to have this conscience-demanded and officially sanctioned education for their children looks like a freedom to have the impossible. It is like freedom to live on the moon. It is as if the State should go to elaborate trouble to declare that a man has the right and freedom to nurture a child whom, in fact, he will never be able to nurture. A freedom which cannot be implemented is not much good.

The poorer families—and this means millions of them—do well to be able to pay taxes for the support of one type of school, and thus, no matter how much their freedom is declared and how much their conscience may hurt, they can scarcely exercise freedom of choice in education. They

are in fact bound to send their children to schools not of
their choice.

This important point was well made by the late Canon
Bernard Iddings Bell, who was assistant to the Episcopal
bishop of Chicago. Here are his words:

But, it may be asked, if only the public schools are state-
supported, if to send children to a school not state-run is possible only at an extra cost beyond the means of most citizens,
is the usual parent not in effect coerced to accept the public
school even against his conscience? Where is the liberty
guaranteed by the Constitution? It would seem to be liberty
almost impossible for the poor and reserved for the financially
better off.

Evidently, then, the problem is a serious one in our
national educational life. Parents are obliged to send their
children to school, and if they wish, they may send them
to church-related schools. What is the strength of saying
"they may" and "if they wish"? Back of it, at least in
theory, is the most important of all freedoms—the freedom
of conscience. Their conscience tells some parents that
they ought to send the children to such schools. In practice,
however, some of them are too poor to do so, and in effect
are coerced into sending their children to schools which
their conscience disapproves.

Against such coercion, there are two indefeasible laws.
One is the law of freedom of conscience. We never have
the right to invade and coerce conscience, not even in the
case of the worst criminal. The inviolability of this law is
granted by all parties to any possible dispute in the matter,
by Jews, Catholics, Protestants and secularists. The other
law is that of the United States of America. The federal
Supreme Court said in *Pierce* that Americans are never to

try forcing parents so that their children must receive instruction from public schools only. Here are the significant words of that decision: "The fundamental theory of liberty upon which all governments in this union repose excludes any general power of the State to standardize its children by forcing them to accept instruction from public teachers only." The same was said by the American Catholic hierarchy (Nov. 20, 1955): "Private and church-related schools exist, not by sufferance, but by right. The right is implicit in the whole concept of American freedom and immunity from totalitarian oppression and in the constitutional framework of our Federal government and of the several states."

Commanded by the State to send their children to school, and commanded by conscience to send them to schools they can ill afford—that is the parents' dilemma.

Conscience will not allow it, and the law of the land will not allow it—that is yet another dilemma. The "it" to which we refer is a coercing and forcing of poor parents, unable to pay for schools of which their conscience approves, to send their children to schools of which their conscience does not approve. To coerce and force in this regard would be like coercing and forcing poor people to suffer abortion, sterilization and euthanasia because they are poor. In all such instances, the theory would seem to be that poor men must give up the most basic freedoms.

In the instance of freedom of choice in education, the *Pierce* decision said that all parents may exercise this freedom. What we are asking is whether this declared freedom is perhaps vacuous and empty.

Put the situation in this way. People may have private schools. But because of financial problems, many of those schools might have to be inferior and to do inferior work.

That is one option: Americans would bargain for freedom of choice in education, but with a permanent condition of inferior academic results for the several million children whose parents would choose private schools. A second option would be to give up, to have to give up, freedom of choice in types of schools. The third option—there are only three—would be to grant some financial aid, at least for limited purposes, to private schools.

The primary issue is the effective right of parents to educate their children as the parents deem proper, and the immediate practical problem is to remove any actual infringement on this right. The actual infringement is complicated; it is at once psychological, moral, political and financial.

By this time in our argument, it has become evident that in the field of freedom for religious education, we have not yet worked out anything like an adequate national policy and practice. What we must eventually achieve is a policy and practice providing for effective freedom of conscience and belief, and this is another way of saying that we must find ways to work out adequate provision for a thoroughgoing educational pluralism.

Freedom Is Divisive

It is difficult to go fully with pluralism in education since it means perpetually achieving unity within an assured diversity. The diversity side is the freedom side, and it is this that naturally gives rise to the problem of divisiveness and the charge of fragmentation. Hence we must inquire whether private schools, church-related or others, are divisive and, if so, whether in a really evil sense. We treat the subject under four headings.

First, the one considerable and convincing study available on the subject, that by Peter and Alice Rossi (in *Daedalus*, v. 90, Spring 1961, pp. 300–328), said that it found no evidence that citizens educated in Catholic parochial schools are less community-minded than their neighbors. What the Rossis reported is that these citizens have not been divided from or torn away from community participation by having been educated in Catholic parochial schools. The Rossis brought together data from several social-science studies, notably studies made in New England by the Harvard University graduate school of education and a study which covered most of Florida. The conclusions from the combined studies are of much interest on the "divisive" and other issues, and are contrary to popular opinion. Here are the conclusions:

. . . we could find no evidence that parochial schools tend to alienate individual Catholics from their communities. Parochial-school Catholics are as involved in community affairs as anyone else of comparable occupational position. Furthermore, the choice of parochial-school education is apparently not so much a rejection of the public schools as a choice of something qualitatively different. It would appear that an improvement of the public schools would not materially affect their attractiveness to Catholics, for the greater pull of Catholic schools is based on religious qualities which the public schools have deliberately avoided. . . . We have been unable to find evidence that parochial-school Catholics are very different from other Catholics.[1]

A second way to consider the question of divisiveness is to ask whether certain well-known Americans educated at private schools have been less community-minded and American than others educated at public schools. On the

[1] *Op. cit.*, pp. 323–324.

private education side take Washington, Jefferson, the two Roosevelts and Kennedy, and on the other side take Truman and Eisenhower. Would men such as those in the former bracket have been more American if educated in public schools, or men like those in the latter group have been less American if educated in private and church-related schools? Or put the present question in another way: Would we want all Americans educated in a monolithic set pattern? Is that what people mean when they urge that, in order to avoid divisive effects and to attain a more perfect union, all children should be educated in public schools and none in independent schools?

Our third observation takes the bull by the horns and says that, of course, private and church-related schools are divisive. In this regard, they are like public schools. Our assertion means three obvious things: first, that the children in private schools are not in public schools—and vice versa: secondly, that children in private church-related schools are presumably introduced to some areas of knowledge and understanding not open to children in public schools, hence the gap and the inevitably divisive effect of each type of school and each type of education; and lastly, that children in either the public or the private schools, church-related or other, may get the notion that they are superior, the only good people, the elect, the prime patriots or even, beyond others, the children of God. We have thus to conclude that private schools are divisive and that public schools also are divisive. The divisive issue cuts both ways.

The trouble with the claim that private schools in particular are divisive is therefore twofold: that the assertion is jejune because platitudinous, and that it is not very circumspect.

Freedom is divisive. This is true of freedom of choice in

education and of every freedom a man can practice. And that, incidentally, is why the problem of pluralism occurs in society—because men and groups have freedom of thought, of beliefs, of association, of action. That is the freedom half of the pluralistic situation, and, by itself, this freedom half—which is basic and essential—is divisive and raises problems. In Lord Acton's formula, "Liberty provokes diversity, and diversity preserves liberty."[2]

The other half is the unitive half, which demands that men and groups, in education and in every social enterprise, bend their freedoms to some common goals of good. Left to itself, freedom is hardly a unitive factor. As Bishop Wright of Pittsburgh has remarked, for anyone to speak on any debatable issue is "to divide the community." Such is the normal effect of freedom. The freedom of Baptists to believe as they will, the freedom of a man to have his own wife and family, the freedom of a person to privacy— these and like freedoms are not primarily unitive forces in society. Hence those arguing against private schools as divisive, if they mean divisive in a pejorative sense, should, in order to be consistent, argue against Jews saying their own prayers in their own homes or synagogues and against a man having his own house and family.

A fourth way, quite realistic, too, to look at the "divisive" challenge is to note, as many have noted, that a school founded on the parish basis is commonly more mixed and heterogeneous socially than is the public school. It is less mixed, of course, in matters religious. But as a rule a parish in America cuts across social and status levels, so that a parish school is likely to contain children at once from the somewhat elite side of the parish and from the middle

[2] Lord Acton, *Essays on Freedom and Power* (New York: Meridian Books, 1955), p. 160.

classes and from the poorer side or even the slum side, and in that way it is socially more democratic than the average public school even in the same city. This is a phenomenon that Leo Pfeffer, no friend of religion in schools, has noted; he has said that the homogeneity usually characteristic of public schools is "far less prominent" in parochial schools, whose children "are more likely to be of different social, economic, racial and ethnic origins."[3]

Granting an inherent divisive factor in freedom, and therefore in freedom of choice in education, there remain many values in this freedom of choice. For one thing, it helps toward some "cultural distinctiveness" which, says Professor Robert D. Cross, of Columbia University, is of "immense importance in the maintenance of a liberal, pluralist society in America." Among ways to do this, Dr. Cross believes, is to allow "various groups to educate their children as far as possible in the direction that *they*, not the state, the majority or the educational theorists, think best."[4]

The weakness in the divisive allegation is that it is unreal and confused and far from circumspect. It fails to observe the actual pluralist situation, rests on a fundamental misunderstanding of freedom, and is not only a refusal to encourage freedom, but a refusal to accept the ordinary effects of freedom. Among the inevitable effects is some distinction—division, dividedness, divisiveness—into free groupings: in family life, ownership, religion and education. Obviously, this freedom and its consequent distinction can be overworked; and an overworking of it in education and religion results in what Professor Littell has rightly called "defensive ghettos." These occur among various

[3] Leo Pfeffer, *Creeds in Competition* (New York: Harper, 1958), p. 81.

[4] *Columbia College Today*, Spring-Summer 1963.

groups, and it would be unfortunate, especially in these ecumenical times, to allow either education or religion to develop and promote them. They have already been too long and too far nourished among Jews, Catholics and Protestants.

With so much said and emphasized, we must nevertheless protest that the divisive allegation is so weak in theory and in relation to reality that we were surprised to see it repeated in a "resource document" issued in 1963 by the Department of Religious Liberty of the National Council of Churches. The four main arguments against aid to primary and secondary church-related schools—arguments which the Council published, but for which it did not accept responsibility—were so much on the cliché and unreal side that we suppose the Council must have hesitated in issuing them in its name. In any event, it was said that tax aid for religious schools "should be opposed because," quoting further,

1. it would undermine our historical ideal of separation of church and state;
2. it would violate both federal and state constitutions;
3. it would severely damage, if not destroy, our public school system and our educational standards;
4. it would accelerate the fragmentation of our society and particularly increase religious conflicts.

By this time in our history these arguments are understood by all to be ambiguous, and it is somewhat of a disappointment that the Council brought them out under its imprint. On its own responsibility, the Council said that it was opposed to aid—beyond welfare services—for children in primary or secondary religious schools or for the parents of those children; that to have to pay taxes for such aid

would be an infringement of religious liberty; and that aid
would cause fragmentation of public education and destroy
"or at least weaken it" so that it could not possibly do its
work. The Council took no stand against aid to church-
related colleges and universities or hospitals, or to churches,
and thus apparently approved aid to them.[5]

Pluralism and the First Amendment

As all citizens know, the Supreme Court has in recent
years had trouble and acute sufferings with the two clauses
of the First Amendment: "Congress shall make no law respecting an establishment of religion, or prohibiting the
free exercise thereof." These limitations may appear simple.
But events have proved that it is difficult to keep from leaning toward one side or the other—toward favoring some
particular religion almost as if "established," or, on the
contrary, toward being too tough on the free exercise of
religion. Too much freedom or too little freedom is a problem throughout society, in the family, the Church, the
State, the school and the arts; in all areas, men encounter
the problem of nothing too much or too little, above all in
regard to freedom. Ordinarily, this problem of "the mean"
is easily handled. But when it comes down to a decisive
issue, as it occasionally does, there is no rule of thumb to
settle the issue, and Aristotle remarked that any practical
decision must come to the point where, with no further
premises available to it, the practical or prudential judgment has to rest on the individual person's intuition. The
ruler frequently has to make such decisions, and so do the
father of the family and the educator, and so does every

[5] *Public Funds for Parochial Schools?* A Resource Document. National Council of Churches: New York, 1963.

man. The justices on any court have to make decisions, and they too must now and then come down to what is called a hair-line decision. Many are under the impression that the justices on the highest court are guided simply and solely by the law and the Constitution. Sometimes these men cannot be solely so guided, and speaking about the *McCollum* decision, Justice Jackson declared that in this instance the justices had entered a field wherein there was no law or Constitution to serve as guide and where, he said, nothing was left but each man's own "prepossessions."

Actual cases coming to the Court are extremely complicated. That is one reason why keeping the line straight between the first clause and the second, in the troublesome First Amendment, has proved to be a continuing problem.

Then there is a second reason for perplexity in the present case. As the understanding of it in operation has developed, each side of the First Amendment has turned out to be immensely complicated. Just when is a law or a practice tantamount to an "establishment of religion"? And what, after all, is "religion" and what is an "establishment"? Just when and under what detailed circumstances is a law or a practice a genuine favor to a particular religion? These questions have given the Court many headaches. The Supreme Court said, eight to one, that the practice then current (1948) at Champaign, Illinois, of the teachers of various religions entering the public school and teaching religion to some students was in effect an aid by the State to particular religions, and was tantamount to an establishment of religion. But in the *Zorach* case four years later, the Supreme Court said in a split decision that the practice of releasing children from school, at the parents' written request, to take courses in religion elsewhere, was not tantamount to such establishment, some justices voting for the side against which they had voted in *McCollum*. It looked like a rightabout-face, and venerable justices hotly said so. Or take another illustration. In 1947 Justice Douglas voted with the majority in *Everson,* holding that it is constitutional and no establishment of religion for the state (New Jersey in the case) to pay tax money to parents as a refund for the money they had spent in transporting their children to parochial schools. Yet the same Justice Douglas said in concurring in the New York prayer decision of 1962 that if he had to do it over again, he would vote the other way in *Everson* (and, further, would abrogate all the deeply entrenched customs of American State and Church collaboration), so that at least to the lay mind it appeared that Justice Douglas could say yes and no to the same question in almost the same breath, and the public was given the no doubt mistaken impression that a man on the highest court could be extremely unstable.

Even by itself, then, the first clause of the First Amendment is seen to be difficult to interpret and apply. The other clause—no interference with the free exercise of religion—is scarcely a simpler matter. It is true that, beginning with *Everson* in 1947 and ever since that time, the Court has appeared to be tough on anything that might so much as remotely look like any aid and official blessing on religion in public schools; it was most notably so in *McCollum,* and *Engel,* and the Lord's Prayer case of 1963. The first of those decisions was the most discussed and was perhaps the most adversely criticized. The late Professor E. Corwin of Princeton University, one of the most distinguished authorities on the Constitution, wrote in a widely circulated article that in *McCollum* the Court was in effect attempting to make itself the national school board.

Nevertheless, cases involving precisely the freedom of

religion have been judged and these, too, are difficult. We previously mentioned the *Barnette* decision allowing children to omit the flag salute in a public school because their parents complained that the act was an invasion of religious freedom, and the several decisions in favor of the Jehovah Witnesses' plea for freedom to preach in public streets and public parks. No doubt these were far from simple decisions to render.

Judgment purporting to give the applied meaning of either clause therefore requires labor and expertness on the part of the Court. What makes the labor greater and the decisions more open to criticism is the fact that neither clause may be taken alone and as if it were a thing in itself, but each must always be taken together with the other. The two clauses have not only to be seen in due and multiple relationships to each other, but the two have to be seen almost as one. The result is that when the Court faces a case involving either clause, it has to be careful which way it moves and is as if obliged to walk a tight rope. The problem is more than to stand solidly with each clause. Respect for the "no establishment" clause, popularly called the "wall of separation" clause, and at the same time for the "no interference" clause, and for the balance between the two—all this, we may confidently predict, will continue to raise an infinity of problems.

The most thorough and useful study on balancing the two clauses is, as mentioned earlier, that by Professor Philip B. Kurland, "Of Church and State and the Supreme Court." Dr. Kurland maintains that the proper construction of the religious clauses in the First Amendment "is that the freedom and separation clauses should be read as a single precept that government cannot utilize religion as a standard for action or inaction because these clauses prohibit classification in terms of religion either to confer a benefit or to impose a burden." That is to say, questions of "separation"—that is, of possible aid to a particular and favored religion—and questions of freedom are inseparable. Anyone suggesting that the answer to these relevant and urgent questions is, as a matter of constitutional law, clear one way or the other is, said Kurland, either deceiving or deceived, and the "seeming simplicity of the 'absolutist' construction of the first amendment is only too patently disingenuous."

The main thrust of the Kurland study was that the two clauses of the Amendment, almost like the two sides of the pluralistic problem—the freedom side and the common good side—must be seen in balance and as *one* comprehensive whole. We use his central idea at this juncture not merely to emphasize that the two clauses of the Amendment, the "no establishment" clause and the "no interference" with freedom clause, must be kept in balance and that a comprehensive view of them must be taken, but also to suggest that the two clauses have some likeness to the two sides of the pluralist principle. It is as if the First Amendment were written to make constitutional provision for the pluralist principle in education, and as if the framers of the Amendment were saying that all must have respect for the freedom of believers, and that believers must have respect for the common good.

The Harvard Report of 1945

In 1945, twelve scholars of Harvard University completed a careful study of general education and made their Report, which is presently being brought up to date. It is interesting to see how solicitous in effect were those twelve scholars to take due account of the pluralist principle in education. Speaking only about the problems of general and unspecialized education—high school and collegiate— the Report said: "Finally, the problem of general education is one of combining fixity of aim with diversity in application." The aim, it was said, was not to provide a general education that would be dead-level uniform for all schools and colleges in the nation, but "rather to adapt general education to the needs and intentions of different groups . . . to adapt a central unvarying purpose to varying outlooks . . . a general education capable at once of taking on many different forms and yet of representing in all its forms the common knowledge and the common values on which a free society depends."

The Report thus said a balance was necessary, and the two sides to be balanced were to be much like the two sides of the pluralist requirements, the common good side and the freedom side. Of course, the Report was using its own terms for these, but notice the similarities: on one hand, fixity of aim, an unvarying purpose, the common knowledge and common values of a free society; on the other hand, diversity in application, the needs and intentions of different groups, an education taking on many different forms.

All this looks to us like a declaration for freedom combined with a declaration for the common educational good, and the combination was something the twelve Harvard men could assume as a desired goal of all education.

8 · What Is Being Done?

A Necessary Negative Step

It is a good thing, no doubt, to make out a case for pluralism in general and for its two important sides and their relation to education. Yet in our present inquiry this general statement is far from enough. In addition, we must proceed to suggest ways in which pluralism can be achieved in American education. These ways are tentatively suggested, and we emphasize that in regard to educational pluralism our complaint is not that we do not have pluralism in education; in fact, we have much of it. Our complaint is that we do not have nearly enough of it, that today our educational efforts are far from utilizing, let alone exhausting, the possibilities of pluralism, and an observer, scanning the field with care, might be forgiven for failure to find half a dozen American educational leaders with a comprehensive view of the actual pluralistic scene in education, let alone of what is pluralistically to be done and could readily be done.

In short, pluralism in American education, though present and effective, is scarcely accepted. In fact, it has in large part yet to be discovered and developed.

These strong statements simply mean that we have few if any leaders who work with our entire educational resources. Leaders are public-school men or private-school men, and seldom are pluralistic schoolmen.

In the circumstances, what could conceivably be done? First of all, from a negative or at best a neutral point of view, educators and other persons and groups with influence on education should stop speaking and acting against whole types of education. They should totally desist from bad talk. To be worthy of continued existence, vast associations such as the National Educational Association have to learn to be circumspect about what they say and do. Any group with such power and prestige has responsibilities to the whole of the national educational enterprise. Even a stand-by and hands-off practice is far from good enough; at a minimum, the big and influential group must, at least in its leaders, know and appreciate the entire educational scene, and if at times and in some matters it cannot work with others, it must know how to be discreetly silent. What we have just said holds, of course, as strictly for associations of private educational groups and their leaders— for instance, for leaders in the National Catholic Educational Association. It is insufficient for the big association, public or private, to be diplomatic; its leaders must know the aims and problems and achievements of every type of school, and must learn to appreciate the total American educational enterprise.

To look on "the other" as an enemy should be an outmoded and primitive attitude, and it is high time to call a moratorium on walls. If at present neither party knows how to work with the other, each must learn how. This is an essential part of its own education and in general of our American education, and it is more important than classrooms or money.

Blasts and counterblasts, obstructionism—any such word or act is absolutely forbidden and should be unforgivable. Lobbying against a body of schools, public, private, technical or general—such a thing could not enter the mind of a man fit to be an educator. Of course, in a vast body of educators, some incredibly narrow spirits will be found and may have to be tolerated. But they have no business dictating national policy.

Persons not engaged directly in education can also have a powerful influence on it. They must accordingly watch what they say and do. A negative roar from one of them, though it might on occasion be needed, ought first to be well considered, since it could do immense national harm. The people who most commonly do this kind of thing are the big churchmen, Protestant and Catholic, and sometimes it seems that, in their tremendous fulminations and counter-fulminations, they have far too little sense for the total pluralistic movement of American education. Of course, it is easy to imagine a situation in which a churchman or a religious body feels that to speak out is absolutely necessary in order to save educational freedoms and rights that must be saved. It seems to us that it was such a situation when, in 1961, Cardinal Spellman spoke out so vigorously against what he took to be the injustice and un-Americanism of saddling on to patrons of parochial schools a federal tax for the sake of public schools only.

Blasts and counterblasts come largely from religious leaders. The worst and most unpardonable come—and keep coming—from the organization called Protestants and Others United. But none of the four major faiths is exempt from this sin. Whether a word or an action is circumspect is a matter of prudential wisdom and decision. But it would be easy to find some Protestant and some Catholic journals of influence which any reasonable committee would have to say have been less than helpful to their educational "enemies." A kind of sadism has kept running through much of the allegedly Christian press and some of the Jewish press in America. To take an outstanding case, think how irresponsible, not to say savage, was *The Christian Century* in its reaction to Cardinal Spellman's position mentioned above.

Considerable religious committees—one would hesitate to say religions—can also be at fault in these matters, and above all in regard to pluralism in education. A few years ago Protestants made a presumably careful study on the delicate and touchy problem of how religion might and could be taught in public schools, which certainly is a common and pluralist problem. When the preliminary report by those Protestants was submitted to various competent persons for suggestions, Dr. John Bennett, of Union Theological Seminary, who is a well-balanced man, said that the report showed a shocking lack of understanding of and sympathy for the position of Catholic schools. Like Dr. Bennett, we were hardly able to conceive that a national body carefully selected and spending some years on the project could so far miss an understanding of and sympathy for a main part of American pluralistic development in education. But a friend who is a Protestant clergyman has reminded us that the failure to see and to love—a failure that is by no means all on one side—is rooted far back in modern history and in pioneer American history, and that the present miscarriage of understanding is the result of the Protestant assumption that ours is a quasi-officially Protestant country; he said that the contrary assumption, essentially involved in a pluralistic view, is even today a sort of affront to the mentality of a remnant of Protestants; hence, he added, the real and honest difficulty they had experienced in believing that anybody except a Protestant could be a trustworthy president. In short, as Professor Littell has pointed out, Protestants did not at first understand or conceive that allowance must be made for pluralistic freedoms, and even today the allowance may be difficult. We have every reason to suppose that in largely Catholic countries, Catholics often proceed on corresponding monistic and anti-pluralistic assumptions.

A similar block develops in other areas, such as race. Suppose that the man best qualified to be governor of Mississippi or Alabama was Negro. Could the white population make allowance for the pluralistic freedoms that would make his election a reality? In the field of race and that of religion, the moral failure is one of justice and charity, and the political failure is a refusal of freedom and effective democracy.

Ill-advised and intemperate words and actions, therefore, on the part of churchmen, educators or associations, can be intelligible, given our various histories. At the same time, we should be slow to condone them, and all are bound as if by contract to work to exorcise them.

Released Time

Much more important is the positive and constructive side of the pluralistic situation, and we could scarcely exaggerate its possibilities. If we could get relatively rid of obstructionists, we would only have reached a neutral ground, and at that point we would have to begin to work together. What are the possibilities in regard to religious education in and through schools, public and private, and what are some of the things that can be done?

Actual pluralistic cooperation between Church and State in education is afforded by various techniques, among which we shall first consider released time. According to the *Zorach* decision of 1952, the child may be released from school, at the parents' written request, to attend religious instruction off the school premises. New York State allows and, under certain stipulations, requires one released hour a week, and Indiana allows two hours, for this instruction.

To discover whether released time amounts in general to much education in matters religious would require a special inquiry. However, we know from observation that in some places the instruction of Catholic children on released time has been remarkable; for example, in Fairport, New York, and in Ithaca, each of these two cities having *a school of Catholic religion collaborating with the public school*. Yet, whatever its merits, this is far from an easy technique to operate. Good work through released time takes much care and planning, on the part of superintendents of both the public and the church-related schools, and on the part also of teachers in the public schools, who, to a notable extent, are thereby incommoded. Nevertheless, grant that it does take good will and some disturbing readjustments. Much is always required by education and especially by freedom and a general pluralism in education. As we insisted, pluralism allows generously for freedoms but asks all parties to bend their freedoms to an over-all common good. A released-time program is cast perfectly in the pluralistic role, balancing the freedom side with the common good side. Still, it is an awkward technique to manage and, since the Supreme Court only permits it but would never be likely to require it, whether it will catch on to any great extent remains a question. Also we must hesitate in predicting that at best it could be expected to do great good, to reach any heights or depths, or to work out into any considerable and creative educational values.

Shared Time

In the procedure becoming so widely and favorably known under the name of "shared time," the child, primarily under the control of his parents and at their choice, attends a public school part of the time—say, a part of each day or each week—and a private or perhaps a church-related school part of the time. The time is shared, and the schools and teachers and equipment are shared—and all of this at the discretion of the parents and presumably for the good of the whole educational life of the child, and thereby of the community and the nation. The idea is that the parents are thus enabled to secure exactly what they want: their child's education in what is often called secular matters (for example, in mathematics or physics) and also in a religious and, if the parents so choose, a sectarian understanding of man and God. Obviously, the operation of shared time has to be thoroughly pluralistic.

Many suppose shared time is totally new. However, shared time has actually been in use in various places and in varying degrees; it has operated for twenty years in Connecticut. An Iowa small city has had shared time in operation for several years with no fuss and fanfare, students from the Catholic high school, if their parents so wish, receiving instruction in biology and chemistry at the public high school. When *Religious Education* said in its January-February 1962 issue that the first published statement on shared time was by Harry L. Stearns in *Christianity and Crisis* for September 1961, the assertion might have been correct, though the practice long antedates that statement. Happily, himself a believer in freedom harmonized with the common good, Mr. Stearns puts the meaning of shared time in this simple fashion: a sharing of the school time of children between state-supported and church-supported schools, the former supplying general education in a religiously neutral context and the latter in a denominational religious context. The basic assumption, as Mr. Stearns points out, is that the child is under the control of the parents, who, though they must meet the State's requirement that the child be educated, may choose what their child's education is to be and who is to provide it.

A challenging and happy feature of Mr. Stearns' statement, and perhaps unnoticed by him, is that he almost literally says that shared time was as if designed to meet the requirements and specifications of pluralism. Here are his words:

> The concept of shared time has developed as a proposed means of bringing the state and the church into a sharing of the time of all children at the discretion of the parents, and it constitutes a revision of the concept that there shall be church schools which claim all the time of some children and public schools which claim all the time of others.

Perhaps we shall soon have vigorous assertions against shared time as, on the one hand, unholy and an invasion of religious liberty and, on the other, as amounting to an unconstitutional establishment of religion. Up to date, however, little if anything is said on either side, and both Catholics and Protestants have applauded the plan. At least as Mr. Stearns proceeds to suggest how shared time might comprehensively work, its affinity is to released time "off the premises," and since this was approved in *Zorach*, shared time may be seen to be constitutionally acceptable. The distinguished constitutional lawyer Leo Pfeffer has said that since, in accordance with the *Pierce* decision, students may receive all their state-required instruction at a private school, presumably they may receive part of it there on a shared time basis; and since the *Zorach* decision allowed literally for released time, the constitutional question is presumed to be already answered.

In Mr. Stearns' scheme, if a community had 4,500 students in primary and secondary public schools and 1,000 in Catholic schools, each of the Catholic students would attend religious teaching in a private school and be enrolled in a public school for part of his schooling, taking some of the burden in numbers and financing and manpower off the Catholic school plant; Jewish students would be free some hours out of the normal school day or week to attend afternoon Hebrew schools; and Protestant students would be free for instruction and ritual in their churches. That is, if and insofar as parents chose the arrangement, the whole plan ideally encouraging freedom for all.

Mr. Stearns, who is a Protestant and is superintendent of public schools in a New Jersey city, is at once philosophical and practical. He says that great numbers of American citizens, "reared in the democratic tradition and largely under religious influence, will accept the view of most church leaders that the child is God's creature, entrusted to parents for nurture." At the same time, these citizens will grant that the Church and again the State has needs and unquestionable rights in the field of education. But a first principle with Mr. Stearns is his insistence that when it comes to rights in education, parents have the priority.

This is the basis of his entire position, and he takes this as the chief difference between released time and shared time. The released time assumption at least appears to be that the State has the primary and even the sole rights over the child's nurture and life, but may on occasion "release" some time to the Church, an assumption rejected by Mr. Stearns. On the other hand, shared time supposes that the child is much more the child of the parents than of the State, and that therefore in education the radical decisions are to be made by the parents; it is their right and duty to decide where and by whom the child will be educated, and, in case they send him to a public school, they may decide whether his whole school day and his whole formal education are to be commandeered by the public school.

Though it is never so in intention, it is possible that the public school sometimes is in reality destructive of our religious ways of life; for instance, by its silence, and even perhaps on occasion by its inability or—as a man in a teachers' college asserted—its lack of freedom to cover adequately the theological content encountered everywhere in context in the humanities. At least on the high school level, shared time might do something to give Catholics and Protestants and Jews a chance to make up this national deficit suffered by the public school's inability to meet the problem of instruction in theological matters.

Though somewhat inchoate and experimental today, shared time is showing promise in several communities. For instance, selected and topflight students from a Catholic high school in Pittsburgh attend that private school where they are engaged in receiving instruction in the elements of theology and in some other value laden subjects. Concurrently they avail themselves of the opportunity to take classes in certain technical areas such as chemistry, marketing and computer programs in a public high school which, for those studies, has far better equipment and stronger manpower than the private Catholic school could readily afford. (In regard to scientific equipment, the federal arrangement is loans to private schools versus outright grants to public schools.)

This particular Pittsburgh public high school is not only select—in faculty, equipment and students—but it serves several school districts, within one of which the students from the Catholic school reside. It is a "break," too, that these students, attending their public school from 7.30 to 10.30 a.m., may ride the school bus, and that they also ride the bus away from that public school to another which happens to be near their private school. But even if in piloting a shared time project not all schools would be so fortunately located, it is perhaps possible that, with much careful planning and with fine pluralistic cooperation, scores of places could work out something comparable to this Pittsburgh plan, which up to now appears so feasible.

The superintendent of schools for the Pittsburgh diocese names these among the advantages of the actually shared time:

1. It gives the church-related school the chance to achieve an effective education for all its children. The general situation in many places today is that a good half of the Catholic children have to be turned away from Catholic schools for want of room. For instance, in the diocese of Rockville Center, New York, 9,000 children are now in Catholic high schools, and four new schools being built will accommodate at least another 9,000; but the two figures combined add up to less than half the Catholic high school children in the diocese, and it is predicted that by 1970 the diocese will have 70,000 Catholic high school boys

and girls. Thus for the majority of Catholic or Protestant or Jewish children, shared time might be the only chance to receive a thorough religious and theological instruction. Otherwise, most Americans must remain illiterates theologically.

2. All children of all faiths could, if their parents wished, receive a religiously oriented education.

3. The system invites all to a pluralistic working in education and affords public and private educators a good and needed opportunity of learning to work together.

4. The money expended in this procedure goes either to the student or directly to the public school, and for that reason no complaint could arise about possibly aiding a church.

The director of the public high school in the Pittsburgh case is also happy with the plan. He points out that, in this plan, inaugurated in the autumn of 1962, the students from the Catholic school come from one of twenty-two districts served by his school: "They're students from a particular school district. . . . We're worried about education. Children need the education we're in business to impart. They're the sons and daughters of taxpayers, and this school is set up for taxpayers' children. They're entitled to the education; our sole concern is that it be available to them."

Bishop Wright, of Pittsburgh, has remarked that in the public-private debate, it is frequently forgotten by educators and politicians that "the public schools belong to all the citizens and are subject to their good pleasure. They do not belong to educational associations nor to pressure groups."[1]

[1] See John G. Deedy, "Shared Time—the Pittsburgh Area's Experiment." *Ave Maria*, March 2, 1963.

Learning Theology at Home

One of the popular ways to dispose of how to teach matters religious and theological to American children is to say that homes and churches should do the task and leave all other teaching to the public school. Such was the suggestion of President Kennedy, and it has been that of many others.

This reply suggests a neat division of labor, but it is a serious question whether the reply is not too simple and whether at bottom it is really a reply at all. We say that it does not begin to face the problems.

For one thing, the churches directly reach only part of the population, and thus, although churches could conceivably do the work for a part, the other large part of our people would have to remain theologically illiterate, and for that reason could not receive anything like a thorough introduction to Western history, let alone to world theology, and would have little chance to enter into man's efforts to achieve wisdom. Besides, the churches, seeing their members only once a week, might at best be able to render them only semi-literate in theology. The following remarks by the late Canon Bell seem scarcely too strong: "Nor will it do—and thinking parents are aware of it—to be content to send the children to neighboring catechism or Sunday school, for, with brilliant but rare exceptions, such well-meant schools are unbelievably bungling and inept; and anyhow, what can be done even by the best of them in an hour or two a week?"[2]

Cannot the home, nevertheless, take up the slack and

[2] Bernard Iddings Bell, *Crisis in Education* (New York: Whittlesey House, 1949), pp. 140–141.

teach a basic theology? The question answers itself. Some homes can; but the ordinary American home is ill-prepared to teach anything like an introduction to theological knowledge. The parents are too busy, and too worn out, to teach the rudiments of any science. They could not teach geography, or geometry, or geology—and who will say that the first steps in any of these areas are more difficult than the first steps in theology? If the home is to teach an introduction to any studies, it might make more sense for the parents to teach the child how to read and write and cipher, since these arts are simpler and are perhaps better in hand on the part of the ordinary American couple than is theology.

Many parents can and no doubt many do teach their children the rudiments of religious practice, how to go through the paces of leading a faithful Hebrew or Christian life. Perhaps we may say that most parents know how to teach children to pray, and do in fact teach them that they are to love and fear God. This is all to the good, and can furnish a practical lore that at least the public schools and colleges are in no position to teach. At the same time, this know-how or practical knowledge, which is as much "religion" as the ordinary couple can teach, leaves the child, and therefore the adult and the populace, without an intellectual grasp or understanding of the acts performed in mankind's religious life.

In other words, a person can hardly be expected to receive an introduction to theological knowledge through the best that the ordinary home and the ordinary church—Jewish or Christian—is giving and is able to give the child today in America. The negative upshot is twofold: first, that a home and church introduction to theology is inadequate; second, that the home and church answer to the problem is far from an adequate answer.

What, then, could be done? Are all hands tied—in other words, is it possible to do anything positive? The answer need be neither recondite nor formidable. In its essentials, it is twofold. First, all lovers of the child, the nation, and of wisdom, will do whatever they can to encourage and aid those who do establish and maintain schools and colleges and universities equipped and free to teach theological knowledge. Far from opposing the church-related institutions, we should all be for them. Our assumption here, of course, is that all of us profoundly believe in freedom and in basic knowledge. How we might well encourage and aid church-related institutions, when and in which particulars we should encourage them, how far and in what ways we might advisedly aid them financially— these are prudential questions which can be answered only by considering ever-changing circumstances. The proposition which goes without saying is that we all should encourage and aid them. Otherwise, we renege on our belief in freedoms and knowledge.

The second "how to do it" is also radically important in a democracy. We should all be receiving some introduction to each others' theologies, and this should be occurring in both the private and church-related and the public institutions, and it could ideally be received on any or all levels. It is shocking, once we come to think of it, that Jews and Catholics and Lutherans live in close proximity and yet no one of the three groups has any justified and clear view of the deepest principles by which the others live. It is not only shocking, but is an intolerable situation because it blesses radical ignorance and is based—so we must suppose—

on obscurantism. Homes and churches do not and cannot supply a break-through to the necessary knowledge. And so we must either remain in ignorance and obscurantism, or our schools of all types—preferably cooperating on how this can be done—must help to bring us out of this primitive condition.

It is true that if a Lutheran is to learn something of Catholic or Jewish theology, most likely he will learn only *about* this theology. That is, he does not *live* the Catholic or Jewish way of life, and the object to be learned—namely, the others' theologies—does not become so thoroughly one with him and so "connatural" to him as does his own lived Lutheran theology. Yet, in a highly pluralist society, we as educators are inexcusable if we do not afford the religionist of any central and basic type the chance and cordial invitation to begin to learn what it is that others believe.

Therefore, in this treatise we are standing foursquare for those in any of the major faiths—for example, the small but increasing numbers in elite Confraternity of Christian Doctrine classes—getting some introduction to what it is the other faiths believe. To proceed any longer in neglect of this introduction is to proceed on a principle of a consciously willed ignorance.

To begin to achieve the needed end of knowing and appreciating each other's beliefs will take the pluralistic planning and pluralistic working together of all educators and all men of good will. An object deeply buried for generations and so deeply buried that it is not noticed at all and is not known to exist is going to be hard to unearth. The chief object in this case is a deep and commanding sense of how desirable it is that all should know something of the faith-principles by which their neighbors live.

What Thomas Jefferson said in this connection should

keep ringing in our ears. Far from excluding theology from the University of Virginia, which he founded, Jefferson consciously made a place for theology; and far from approving theological illiteracy, he said these words: "The want of instruction in the various creeds of religious faiths existing among our citizens presents, therefore, a chasm in a general instruction of the useful arts." If this sentence made sense in his day, it may be thought to make even more sense now, and for two reasons. First, on the part of the faiths. The Protestant faiths have proliferated and, for that reason, it takes more conscious effort to know them, and at least the Catholic and Jewish faiths have become increasingly important in American life. Second, on the part of the time spent in school. The young American of today spends at least six times more years in school than Lincoln did, and it would be inexcusable to leave him after all illiterate in the theological lore of mankind.

9 · What Can be Done?

Learning from Free Nations

Many nations have had and do still have more freedom to use tax money as aid to religious schools, either partly or wholly, than America has today. An example of this is Holland; Canada is another, and England a third. In these and other nations, the people are less afraid of religious doctrines in schools than we are, and their religious groups are less afraid of and suspicious of each other than are our groups. This greater fear and suspicion on our part and lesser one on their part naturally have historical and therefore psychological roots which it would be of great importance to explore. Meantime, we have much to learn from such nations, and we should at least be ashamed if we were unwilling to learn it.

It is easy to complain that the Dutch or the Canadian or the English pluralistic educational system does not work as well as ours does. But this is said by those poorly acquainted with those systems. As an over-all reply to the objection—and this reply was made by a Dutch senator to an actual American objector—we are happy to cite the words of this senator, whose politics and religion are unknown to us and, in any event, are irrelevant to the situation. This is what he said:

To the Editor of The New York Times:

In a letter, Ralph H. Lane refers to the case of Holland in arguing against equality of aid to public and private schools.

He is correct when he says that the Dutch agreed to subsidize all schools equally. In 1920 the decision was made by the Protestant, Catholic, Liberal and even Socialist political parties. They would make the same decision again.

But Mr. Lane is wrong when he states that those schools under Roman Catholic auspices "took full advantage, with the result that Protestant and others in self-defense did the same thing." No well-informed Dutch Protestant or 'others' would agree with Mr. Lane on this point.

Mr. Lane is also correct when he states that "today 30 per cent of the municipalities have no public elementary school." But he overlooks the fact that out of a thousand Dutch municipalities 250 are nearly 100 per cent Protestant. They do not want public elementary schools.

It is true that in 1958 barely a third of the secondary schools and pupils were part of the public school system. But the only conclusion to be drawn from this fact is entirely to the credit of the Dutch system, which gives an equally fair chance to both public and private schools.

Indeed, as Mr. Lane says, teachers and parents also are organized according to creed or point of view. But this can be done in any democratic country and should not lead Mr. Lane to conclude that "there is virtually no communication among schools of the same level in the same town."

Actually communication is very common between administrators and teachers in these schools and even more so among those responsible at the national level.

Mr. Lane speaks of "nuns and brothers who earn standard salaries, which usually they must surrender to ecclesiastical authorities." I understand that Mr. Lane does not object to equal pay. During the Nazi occupation salaries of these teachers were reduced 40 per cent; immediately after the war this measure was abolished by the Dutch Government.

If Mr. Lane of his free will—and such is the case with the nuns and brothers—wishes to spend his entire income supporting some religious institution, nothing in the American Constitution forbids this, provided he pays his income tax. This is also true of the Dutch Constitution, and no one in Holland sees anything wrong with this.

Mr. Lane speaks of a Dutch friend who told him that "the secret of America's greatness is the cosmopolitan public school." I should like to remind this friend that there is a Dutch greatness, too, as every American who does us the pleasure of visiting our country may notice. Perhaps the secret of this greatness lies in the fact that no energy is wasted on discussing the effects of state-supported private schools.

JOHN H. M. DERKSEN,
SENATOR

The Hague, March 23, 1961

To learn about the possibilities as well as the hazards in education on a democratic basis, our leaders in education, and all those—for example, politicians and clergymen—having notable influence on educational policy and procedure must examine honestly and scientifically what is being done in at least such nations as Holland, Canada and England. We keep a large proportion of students in school a longer time, but do we also "educate" our people better? More relevantly to the problems of this book, do we afford youths a better chance to get an introduction to the theological thinking of at least the Occident?

We may doubt that the balance is in our favor. In fact, some nations seem to be more daring in this area and more experimental than our own—and, frankly, more democratic and free; and if this is so, perhaps it is because some of them are more mature than we. The 1961 study by Benjamin Sacks, *The Religious Issue in the State Schools of England and Wales, 1902–1914*, is really an eye-opener, since the English and the Welsh systems officially promote a wonderful democracy and freedom of choice in education.

In this regard, our recommendation is a simple one. It is to visit, read and study, and see if it is possible to learn from the efforts, sufferings, successes and failures of other nations. Presumably we want freedom, democracy and quality in our own total sacrifices for education, and the experience of other democratic nations may assist us in finding the best way.

How, and How Much?

A practical question is sure to be asked in case aid is to be given to private schools. How is this to be done if at all, and in which forms if any, and how much? Though we take these questions regarding a bill of particulars to be somewhat peripheral to our central inquiry, we suggest tentative replies.

First and last, we would say that if aid is to be given, it should be given, whatever the amounts and kinds, to children or their parents and not directly to schools. We have no concern to aid private or public schools, but we must have a concern to protect freedom and to aid children and the national good. In line with this basic principle, the following suggestions are made, and always on the supposition that federal aid is needed and desirable—a question which we waive.

First. Aid should cover the ordinary welfare services,

and this part of it should be what is called child-benefit aid; for instance, hot lunch, free milk, dental services, medical attention, polio shots, transportation, and textbooks in non-religious areas. All such matters are now sanctioned, either by Supreme Court decree—in the case of transportation and textbooks—or by common practice and acceptance; those holding against them belong at best to an outmoded American past. Modern conditions and practices demand these benefits on a non-discriminatory basis.

Second. Scientific equipment, and so forth. This type of aid goes at present in the form of grants to public high schools, but only as loans to private schools. To avoid discrimination and to promote the good of the child and the nation, it should either go in the same form to private and church-related high schools or be cancelled. It is the child and the nation we are helping, and it would be an ineffective and bad policy to do this for only preferred children, to hold back and do it only in a half-hearted and compromised way. To believe or not to believe in the child and the nation—that is, so to speak, the question.

Third. If aid is given—say, for scientific equipment or for textbooks—the public as giver has the right and duty to see how it is used. As matters now stand, the State has some control — loosely exercised, indeed — over church-related schools. Regarding control, we mention two points: it is far from novel, and the idea or theory of it must be granted by all to be entirely reasonable.

Fourth. Should aid also be extended to grants to build classrooms? This question is in a slightly different category from the question of bus service or secular textbooks. For one thing, there is no court decision on it as there is on the two matters just named, though we do have positive legislation on it in favor of classrooms for non-religious classes in church-related schools. Classrooms for science, scientific laboratories—these might possibly be regarded as aids to secular learning, and, in that light, it might fall within a wise state or federal policy to supply them—on a grant basis and not a mere loan basis—to church-related schools. It would be exceedingly unwise to blight the chance of gifted youths to develop in science. It would shortchange both the child and the nation and even the international good. We do not want to do this; and if we deliberately did it, our action would be immoral.

Fifth. But how far, after all, will certain church groups go in asking for aid? If aid X is provided, will Baptists and Catholics and Jews not then ask for aid Y? Would not any aid at all be "an opening wedge"? These are questions that only a dogmatist would answer in an apodictic manner. The closest thing we have to a reply is on the part of Catholics; this is in two statements made by the administrative board of the National Catholic Welfare Conference. First, in 1945 this board said that, not basic subsidy, but merely auxiliary services and child benefits were asked. (Speaking for himself, Cardinal Spellman said this: "Under the Constitution, we do not ask nor can we expect public funds to pay for the construction or repair of parochial school buildings, or for the support of teachers or for other maintenance costs.")

The bishops thus made a strong pledge. But the statements by that board do not necessarily bind any bishop at all, and much less do they bind the American Catholic public, lay and clergy, at all places and into an indefinite future. The words were a policy statement; and, of course, what may be good public policy—for State or Church or school, or their interrelations—at one time, might at another time be unfortunate public policy.[1] In the realm of changing social realities, eternal and absolute dogmas are, as we have emphasized, perilous and should be used sparingly by courts or educators or churchmen.

It may, for instance, some day—and that day may be to-day—be a good and proper thing to use state or federal funds to help staff church-related schools for Cubans pouring into Florida, or for the vast armies of Spanish-speaking in many states. A once-for-all national dogma outlawing any such thought would be a deadend.

What, then, are we to say is the Catholic position on aid to religious education? Strictly speaking, there is no "Catholic position." Some Catholics, including some bishops, are opposed to federal aid to any schools, public or private. The nearest approach to a Catholic position is the rather generally asserted view that if there is to be federal aid to primary and secondary schools, the aid should be "across the board." This means that if federal aid is going to be used for child benefits and welfare services, then aid for these benefits should go to all schools—say, all primary and secondary schools, or to all schools in impacted areas—without discrimination. This is because the aid is not for the school, but for the good of the child, whatever his color or creed, and for the good of the nation, and because it would be a mistake to cut off our nose to spite our face. It means, too, that if aid is going to build and equip laboratories, this aid also should be without any shadow or taint of discrimination. Again, we are interested in the good of the child and the nation, and a half-hearted doing of the job will by no means suffice.

[1] Our remarks are in agreement with those by Neil G. McCluskey, S.J., *Catholic Viewpoint on Education* (Garden City, N.Y.: Hanover House, 1959), pp. 179–183.

This brings us to the second statement issuing from the administrative board of bishops of the National Catholic Welfare Conference. When in 1961 President Kennedy delivered his first message to Congress on education, he spoke to the press and gave a sort of fillip to freedom and democracy in these somewhat autocratic words: "There isn't any room for debate." In any event, debate has continued, and the bishops' board said these four things, which, by the way, might at this or that point leave room for debate. First, whether there should be federal aid must be settled on the basis of objective study of the schools of the nation. Second, if there is to be federal aid, "we are deeply concerned that in justice Catholic school children should be given the right to participate." Third, the bishops thought it constitutional that loans be made to private schools. Fourth, if an aid program were enacted excluding children in private schools, "these children will be the victims of discriminatory legislation. There will be no alternative but to oppose such discrimination."

We repeat, then, that those looking for an "official Catholic position" on aid to schools will look in vain.

If aid is to be given, how could this be done? By what device or technique? We think this is a question outside the limits of our study. We would refer the inquirer to any of several good sources; first, to what is done in other nations in this regard—perhaps England or Holland; and then to those who have made a special study of the problem—for example, Professor Milton Friedman, of Chicago University, and also his colleague, Professor Procter Thomson.[2]

[2] Milton Friedman, "Role of Government in Education" in *Economics and the Public Interest,* edited by Robert Solo (Rutgers University Press, 1955). Procter Thomson, "Educational News and Editorial Comment," *School Review,* XLI (April, 1955).

Briefly, the Friedman plan would be this: A government could give parents vouchers redeemable for a specified maximum sum per child per year if spent (but only if spent) on approved educational services, and the parents would then be free to spend this state-vouched sum and any additional sum to purchase educational services from an approved institution of their choice; and this, of course, was the very plan used with such simplicity and success for veterans under the GI bill.

The Thomson plan offers an alternative: "A public grant could be given to privately operated schools as such, or a certificate could be issued to the individual family which it would be free to spend at a school of its own choosing."

What the family or the child would receive would, in either plan, not be money at all, but a guaranteed freedom of choice in education, something that the family or child does not have today.

The most elaborate plan as to "how" to do it and "what" to do is that of Senator Abraham Ribicoff, of Connecticut, and, though it is proposed as tentative, Senator Ribicoff has repeated it so often, in and out of Congress, that all should be familiar with it. The plan breaks into the following six parts:

First. Income tax deductions for college and private school expenses: for the former, up to $1,500 per student per year; and for the latter, up to $100 per child per year.

Second. Public financing of shared time: ". . . an allotment of funds . . . based on the number of public school pupils plus an additional allotment of one-half the rate for public school students for each private student who attends public schools on a shared time basis."

"A combination of these proposals—tax reductions and

shared time—can help resolve the religious controversy in education. There seems to me no question that both these proposals are constitutional and sound public policy."

Third. Assistance for special purposes. "In elementary and secondary schools, there is a wide range of permissible aid in selective areas such as math, science, and foreign language teaching. An important national purpose is being served and religious implications are nonexistent or at least negligible."

Fourth. Teacher training programs: ". . . a variety of ways . . . We now provide summer institutes for teachers of math, science, and foreign languages, and for those in guidance and counseling . . . open to men and women from both public and private schools. Why not broaden the range . . . ?"

Fifth. Auxiliary services "of direct benefit to the child, such as school lunches, health services or bus transportation."

Sixth. Higher education. "I am entirely satisfied that public funds may be used broadly without constitutional question. . . . Students at Harvard, Southern Methodist, Notre Dame, and Yeshiva all have benefited from these funds."

Progressive Freeing from Prejudice

This heading must be taken to express a double negative and a strong positive, and certainly all would want to embrace the idea at once. However, in practice it always turns out to be a troublesome matter, and this for several reasons. At times, we suffer from ideological blocks, such as the positivist dogma that man can learn only empiric facts. We suffer and will long continue to suffer from creedal con-

flicts, from a desire to protect only our own creedal terri-
tories and sometimes with a sort of sadistic desire to attack
and cripple others; also from a dogmatic egalitarianism
which decrees that all must be educated alike and together.
Given the creedal-conflict block and the positivist and the
egalitarian block, it is difficult to free ourselves from our
general religious and theological illiteracy. It will take considerable maturing. Today it would be hard to find teachers generally for either the public or the church-related
schools with sufficient religious and theological knowledge
and freedom so that they themselves would be openminded
and uninhibited and thereby genuinely prepared to teach
religions and theologies.

Let us be concrete on this issue and ask what percentage
of the approximately 90,000 nuns teaching in American
primary and secondary schools is really prepared to teach,
at least in context, the facts of Hebrew worship and the
values in it, or again regarding Lutheran worship and
the values in it? Perhaps hardly one nun in a dozen is so
equipped. Or who will say that the teachers in public
primary and secondary schools, in any village of the Deep
South or any city in the North, can and do communicate,
at least as encountered in context, the facts regarding religion itself, or any particular religion?

Lack of theological knowledge is a progressive ignorance. The teacher in a private or a public school has had
little opportunity to become theologically literate, and now
he is expected, on due occasion as theological questions
arise, to help introduce students to an understanding of
theological matters which he does not grasp; and then
some of his students, becoming teachers, will be called
upon to introduce students of the next generation to those
matters. The children's parents are ordinarily unable to

supply an understanding, and the Sunday sermon and the Sunday school also leave the student untutored regarding the many theological matters he meets in context in grade school and high school.

Speaking of the problem encountered by teachers of arts and literature when they must help students grasp meanings where theology appears in context, Christian Gauss said that secularization in the child's earlier schooling has left a blind spot on the college freshman's mind. "This is equally true," wrote Gauss in *The Teaching of Religion in American Higher Education*, "whether his parents are atheists, agnostics, or still allied to some religious denomination. The competent teacher, whatever his particular faith or lack of faith, finds that without an intelligent grounding in religious concepts, students cannot begin to understand subjects like Gothic architecture or Italian painting, Dante's *Divine Comedy*, Milton's *Paradise Lost*, or Pascal's *Pensées*."

Knowing Each Other

In theory, knowing each other may appear simple, yet in practice it may turn out to be a formidable task. Take the problem of teachers knowing each other across "party lines." Most teaching nuns are somewhat immured in private schools, but do other teachers obviously escape immuring in their schools? All have come to see that political walls can be an evil thing. Are walls between types of schools, and between the teachers in the various types, any longer defensible? Across and around the old walls, teachers must begin to know each other and to work with each other.

If we teachers continue to fail to do so, we are lacking

either in good will or imagination or a patriotic training and spirit. A genuine educator will be imaginative enough, bold enough even, to find ways of crossing artificial lines and man-made walls. By definition, the great educator is a creator and redeemer. Like Plato's demiurge, he has to be building a world, and in building it he is not niggardly or envious. He is magnanimous, so that one corner of the educational world is too small for him. And if what we have just said of the educator is true, it is twice over true of the educational or the academic association—this must be big enough in its leaders to embrace the national educational scene. We have too much in common, and far too much to do *for and with one another*, to remain walled up in private-school or public-school ghettos. This assertion may hurt some people, and if it does, so much the better.

Where, as is so common, there are private and public schools in geographical proximity, the two must come much closer together in understanding and sympathy than they do today. They must learn both how to participate in various common problems and to share and even to pool their learnings. Those who are still afraid of "one world" and of religious unity are living in a dead past.

It is a basic psychological law that nature abhors a psychological vacuum. When persons or groups are near each other in physical fact, there should be between them sympathy, understanding and love. Where these are not present, nature will fill in the vacuum with guesses, suspicions, even with envy, fear and hatred. The types of schools, and again and more importantly their teachers, administrators and students, are too close to each other not to suffer such penalties if and when and insofar as at least the teachers and administrators from the two types fail to mix and, in many matters, to work as one.

At present, there is inter-culturation mainly in athletics; the teams from the parochial schools may perhaps belong to the league—and this, so far, is a good thing—or might even for a price be allowed to play on "school field." In some cases, the superintendents of the two types do meet, at least at formal civic functions; and we know that here and there a superintendent of the public schools or—less likely—of the private schools is willing and anxious to seek ways of working with the total school enterprise of his city.

The old attitude that the twain shall never meet must pass. Teachers and administrators will have to come out of their isolation and go to work on the problem. They will have to do more in this regard than they have yet dreamed of. This is only to say that they must become American, democratic and human. It means joining the human race at the grass-roots level.

At a minimum, they must learn to know each other and sympathize with each other, and this can—so we may surmise—be done at no gigantic cost or sacrifice. But it does take doing; talk and books cannot bridge the gap. This required learning can be acquired only in and by doing. Practical techniques must therefore be devised and tried. An exchange of teachers between the types, for a day or a week or a month, would make good educational sense and could work wonders. This could readily be done, and certainly must be tried. Suppose an exchange, at least for a week or two, of half a dozen nun teachers from their high school with teachers from a public high school. No doubt the idea is ridiculous and shocking, but why is this so? Largely because today we have reached the segregated point where, with school segregated from school and each type ghettoized, we only more or less believe in democracy and pluralism in education.

In the present study, we are omitting for the most part the many problems of pluralism in college and university education, but not because we think that these problems are insignificant or that they will solve themselves. We will merely remark that something considerable is being done, since the church-related colleges and universities have become more and more weaned from the obsession that they possess all knowledge and wisdom and have nothing to learn. However, in Catholic higher learning, whatever of that among Jews and Protestants or secular fundamentalists, an evident persistent weakness has been the rather consistent refusal to participate in national scholarly societies, and this is notably the case in philosophy, theology, social sciences and history.

Working together for the common good is the order of the day. In national and international relations the need for unity is evident and must be met; worldwide pluralistic concepts and practices are demanded. The races likewise must learn to know each other, to sympathize with one another, and to work together, at home and throughout the inhabited globe. The religions must bend their obstinate necks; they must know each other and aid each other—not only Catholic and Protestant, and not only Jewish and Christian, but all religions. This is a worldwide problem. It is high time, too, for capital and labor to commence to understand each other and to find ways, long before troubles start, of working together and playing together.

In the general need for cooperation, educators and administrators of schools cannot be excused for their long delay in this universal task of knowing each other and working with each other. Certainly not! And no longer can we forgive a president, a congress, a supreme court that labors, perhaps on Machiavellian principles, for only one part of American educational enterprise—say, for science only or the humanities only, or for grade schools only or universities only, or for private schools only or for public schools only. In theory and in practice we must learn to come around to the pluralistic and democratic situation and problem. The time has come when ghettos and walls must be knocked down. Suppose the NEA or the Catholic or Protestant or Jewish or secularistic hierarchy does have to join American society, does have to bend and to make terms for the over-all common good! In the educational as well as the cultural field, the United States needs a creative inter-group peace corps.

At all levels, knowing one another would be a good thing. To commence knowing one another would be like a declaration of freedom from ignorance and prejudice. It would be positive, and in line with the best American traditions, since to stand off and form segregated aristocratic groups has always been foreign to us.

In all our efforts to achieve the values of pluralism in American education, and in the use of the techniques at hand, certain readily intelligible suppositions are made. For one thing, we must have men of good will; anything short of this desideratum is useless. Blessed are the pure of heart, for these shall see God. They are able to do this because there is nothing between them and God. It is the same in the needed educational collaboration. The niggardly man with an axe to grind, always looking in a Machiavellian way for his own good or the good of his church or party, is a liability in the immense and complex problems set for educational leaders. Those who are going to do anything will have to be men who are at least relatively free from the party line. And it goes without saying that they will have to be men who believe profoundly in man and in truth and are dominated by charity and justice, men of patience, sure that some things that are impossible today can be done tomorrow.

Men of good will, magnanimous and far-seeing men— these can do much to get us around obstructions and lift us over walls. A man of the quality of John XXIII immediately wins all types and conditions of men. Perhaps we are asking much of Providence when we say, "May his tribe increase among churchmen, statesmen and educators."

For this work, we want men who, for the sake of peace and learning, are willing and anxious to sit down together to consider each other's views and to see how best to meet the national situation. Here are two examples of what we mean. A Protestant leader, Wayne Harvath, director of the Massachusetts Council of Churches' department of social action, though himself opposed to grants to parents of children in religious schools, has urged inter-faith discussion of the problem "with a view to reaching friendly, common understanding of our various positions on this as on other issues." Also the Presbytery of Western New York, though opposed to aid for parochial schools, proposed discussions with Catholics on the subject, and added: "It ill behooves United Presbyterians to stand by without concern for what happens to the parochial school system of their Roman Catholic brethren. United Presbyterians seek discussion with Roman Catholics . . . with a view to finding new and creative solutions to the present public-parochial school dilemma."

On the basis of pluralism, which is the only realistic basis, much can be done. Let us conceive a practical pluralistic first step. Let us imagine a really representative national school board. (We are aware that a national advisory council of education has repeatedly been urged; our interest is in its composition.) The suffering justices on the Supreme Court were never equipped or empowered to be a national school board, and it is unfortunate for them and for many that they have chanced to fall into this role. Far better would be a motion to form an inter-school, inter-faith, inter-racial and non-partisan advisory group to encourage studies and practices in the direction of excellence in education for all our children and youths, with no thought of color or creed or income or country of origin. As Representative Carey, of New York, has proposed, we need a national commission of "men of good will" to work on the issue of federal aid to elementary school children. We would want large-minded men who automatically believe in the freedom of all men. Of course, good men are hard to find, and many of the more virulent statements made on education by partisan and poorly balanced men and even by groups (men and groups with little sense for the democratic and pluralist situation) might make people think that free and just men are rare. However, our own opinion is that the contrary is the case, and we would not hesitate in nominating half a dozen or more of these. The narrow-minded, belligerent monist, seeing only the good of his party or sect, would have to be automatically excluded.

We claim, then, that good men could readily be found. Among Jews, we name at once such men as Rabbi Gilbert, Will Herberg, Walter Lippmann, and Abraham Ribicoff; among Catholics, such men as Cardinal Cushing, Charles Donahue, of Fordham University, John B. McDowell, who is superintendent of schools in the Pittsburgh diocese, and Bishop John J. Wright; and from among many Protestants available, such men as John C. Bennett and Roger Shinn, of

Union Theological Seminary, Paul G. Kauper, of Michigan Law School, and Arthur E. Sutherland, Jr., of Harvard Law School.

Consider the wisdom of an almost off-hand assertion made by a highly placed official of education in Ohio. This man merely made the sane and obvious, yet deeply significant, remark that the public and the private schools have an immense lot in common: common values in large part, much common work to do, and common goals in large part—a platitudinous statement by a man of sense and good will. Consider, too, the following words spoken in 1960 by Rabbi Albert Gilbert, a remarkably well-balanced religious leader, who holds national offices in both Jewish and interfaith societies. As all know, many Jews oppose all instruction in theology in public schools; but speaking to a Baptist convention (shades of Jefferson and "the wall"!) Rabbi Gilbert said these words:

Instead of barring all religion of any sort in the public school we must try to find the techniques that will enable all our religions to be recognized in ways that would not be offensive to anyone. We ought to put our best minds to working on such a program. It is possible, I think, to improve the way we teach about religion where intrinsic to the subject matter. The religious aspects in the culture of our civilization, the religious motivations of the pioneers, the religious dimensions in literature, art, and music, perhaps these can be better taught in our public schools were the best minds of all our religious groups to come together and share the responsibility for pointing the way. A will to reconciliation and a commitment to the creative resolution of interreligious tension—this is what is required of us.

When we come to pluralism in education, the words *we* and *us* have a wide extension. They include all men of

good will in the four major faiths and any fringe faiths,
and also all philosophies and theologies held within American freedoms, and all political parties, and the ways of in-
quiring and of teaching, the levels of education, and surely
the two chief types of education in America.

10 · In Other Words

1. Popular Assumptions on Church, State and School

That there has been and is absolute "separation" in fact.

That "wall" and "separation" are somewhere in the Constitution.

That there is a constitutional difference between high school and college.

That there is a First-Amendment difference between using tax money to support a school and not taxing that school.

That some school-tax money is for the welfare of the student and some is not.

That churches and synagogues are not subsidized.

That public schools are not subsidized.

That it is constitutionally permissible to use tax money to buy scientific equipment for church-related schools, but not permissible to use it to build church-related school-houses.

That the State has *the* priority in education.

That the best national educational policy may advisedly disregard the education of several million children.

That there is effective educational freedom for all the people.

That a school or a school system or a teacher, public or private, can be philosophically and theologically neutral.

That secular education is neutral education.

That democratic values can be inculcated on a neutral basis.

That it is constitutionally wrong for a Protestant clergyman—as has often been and still is the case—to teach in a public school.

That for nuns to teach in a public school is tantamount to an establishment of religion.

That private schools are undemocratic.

That Truman and Eisenhower, who attended public schools, were more democratic and American than Jefferson and F. D. Roosevelt, who attended private schools.

That private schools are divisive, but that private churches and private houses are not.

That public schools are not divisive, and are the only really American schools.

That Americans, being realists, live under no myths—for instance, regarding schools, democracy, the Constitution.

That church-related colleges and universities, in contrast to church-related primary and secondary schools, do only a secular work.

That nations allowing and promoting state aid to church-related schools are less free than we are, and have schools inferior to ours.

That ours are the best schools in the world.

That to criticize the public schools is a misdemeanor.

That the more people there are in school and the longer they stay in school, the better the education.

That the State should make available a college education for all.

That the judgments of the Supreme Court are above criticism.

That public schools are godless.

That minorities, being relatively well treated in America, should silently acquiesce in the *status quo*.

II. Relevant Quotations

"Pluralism is based on a free development of differences." (Charles Donahue, Fordham University)

"There is no academic freedom in Catholic colleges and were Catholics to constitute a majority of the population, education would in all likelihood lose its secular character." (Sidney Hook, New York University)

"And it is hereby declared to be the settled policy of the government to hereafter make no appropriation whatever for education in any sectarian school." (Federal Congress, 1896)

"Catholics are being forced to pay double for the right of freedom in education and are still not getting their money's worth. . . . This is an obvious injustice and a denial of the principle of religious freedom. . . . The First Amendment was intended to limit the powers of federation—not to extend them." (Christopher Dawson)

"As the majority in the *Everson* case pointed out, a state cannot aid religion, but it cannot be denied the right to aid all its children even though some of them attend religious schools." (Robert Fairfield Cushman, Ohio State University)

"A state statute so drawn as to provide aid to all children as a group, regardless of what that aid might be, would be exceedingly difficult to attack on constitutional grounds as an aid to religion. Thus a state which provided medical service and books to all the children in the state would by virtually assured of the validity of its action." (Robert Fairfield Cushman)

"No citizen because of his religion or lack of religion shall be deprived directly or indirectly in theory or in fact of the enjoyment of his rights, privileges or benefits of citizenship nor shall the exercise of the duties of citizenship impair his full religious liberty." (R. J. Henle, S.J., St. Louis University)

"Religion does and should, as part of the public, share in the benefits extended to the public in general. To hold otherwise is to adopt a position which would permit the state to make an outlaw of religion, having no rights which the state is bound to respect." (Robert Fairfield Cushman)

"It is cardinal with us that the custody, care, and nurture of the child reside first in the parents, whose primary function and freedom include preparation for obligations which the state can neither supply nor hinder." (U.S. Supreme Court in *Prince v. Massachusetts*, 1944)

"The greater the proportion of our youth who fail to attend our public schools and who receive their education elsewhere, the greater the threat to our democratic unity." (James B. Conant, ex-President of Harvard)

"The democratic faith is the hardest faith there is . . . opposed to fanaticism, based on compromise, turned toward tolerance, welcoming variety and diversity." (Francis Biddle)

"I fully recognize the justice *in principle* of the Catholic claim to public support of parochial schools, even to the point of contributing to the tuition of pupils and the salaries of teachers; yet I think it would be misconceived to press such claims at the present time or in the foreseeable future." (Will Herberg)

"Strict separation must give way since it would seriously limit the free exercise of religion." (Wilber G. Katz, Wisconsin University)

"If government must leave parents free to send their children to religious schools, does the First Amendment permit the government to respect that freedom further by arranging distribution of its various benefits so as to avoid discrimination against parents or students who make the choice? My answer is yes: such efforts to avoid hostile discrimination do not constitute 'laws respecting an establishment of religion.' " (Wilber G. Katz)

"Learning tolerance for other persons, no matter how different, and respect for their beliefs may be an important part of American education, and wholly consistent with the First Amendment. I hazard the thought that no one would think otherwise were it not for parents who take an absolutist approach to the problem, perhaps encouraged by the absolutist statements of Justices of the Supreme Court, on and off the bench." (Erwin N. Griswold, Harvard University Law School)

"The basic American principle of Church-State relations is not separation but religious liberty." (Wilber G. Katz)

"The State may not compel any form of religious observance. This does not, however, prevent all co-operation between Church and State." (Justice Douglas)

"I am still opposed to any program of Federal aid that would penalize a multitude of America's children because their parents choose to exercise their constitutional right to educate them in accordance with their beliefs. . . . It is not for me to say whether there should be any Federal aid

to education. That is a political and economic matter. . . .
But the Administration's proposal in the field of elementary
and secondary schools is not fair and equitable. It would
limit Federal aid to public schools and thereby withhold
benefits from millions of children attending private and
church-related schools." (Cardinal Spellman)

"Catholic children, even when they attend religious
schools, as they do by constitutional right, must not find
themselves deprived of those benefits which the government of all citizens gives to the children of all citizens."
(Cardinal Cushing)

"If the fact of religion disqualifies citizens of this free
nation from sharing in the benefits provided by their taxes,
it would seem quite clear that some sort of religious test
has been imposed." (Bishop Leo A. Pursley)

"No citizen should be forced to disobey the dictates of
his conscience in order to enjoy the benefits of his citizenship." (George Johnson, Catholic University of America)

"Competing demands by hundreds of church and
private groups for Government subsidies would arise. Tax
subsidy would attract the establishment of an endless
variety of educational systems, duplicating and destroying
the public school system. The principle of separation of
church and state would be in jeopardy." (Protestant Council of the City of New York)

"To deny to tax-paying American citizens of the
Orthodox Jewish faith the benefit of their taxes justly due
to their children is a discrimination which is not in accordance with basic American ideas." (Agudath Israel of
America)

"A singular paradox has emerged in President Kennedy's message to Congress on the use of federal money
for education. While these funds would be authorized to

finance scholarships to students in the college of their choice 'without regard to sex, race, creed or color,' the President says there would be no federal aid to 'nonpublic' schools for construction or teachers' salaries at the elementary or secondary-school level . . . But, it can be argued, if the appropriation of federal money for church schools at the elementary and secondary school level is in violation of the Constitution, why isn't it also unconstitutional to appropriate money for scholarship grants or construction loans to colleges that are denominational?" (David Lawrence, 1961)

"Some government recognition of and backing for religion has been customary for many years and continues with surprising vigor." (Arthur E. Sutherland, Jr., Harvard University Law School)

"It is idle to pretend that this task is one for which we can find in the Constitution one word to help us judges to decide where the secular ends and the sectarian begins in education. Nor can we find guidance in any other legal source. It is a matter on which we can find no law but our own prepossessions." (Justice Jackson, concurring in *McCollum*)

"The wall has no future because it cannot help us learn. If taken literally, it is arbitrary and unreasonable, pretending to separate things that are not in all respects separable, thwarting efforts to understand what education and freedom of (and from) religion demand, hampering us in our search for what we need . . . a national idea of education and a national program to carry it out." (Robert M. Hutchins)

"The question before us is plain: Are the adults of America mature enough to resolve their differences for the education of their children? . . . Sweeping conclusions that there can be no assistance—or that there is no limit to assistance—simply cannot be supported." (Senator Abraham Ribicoff)

"Jefferson believed that the division of human beings into parties was natural and normal. Differences of opinion could not and should not be suppressed. His concept of democracy was actually a system for making controversy creative. The essence of democracy for him was not suppressing controversy, but getting it out into the open and keeping it there until a decision based on common understanding and willing assent had been reached concerning the issue." (Robert M. Healey, University of Dubuque)

"Neither the state nor this Court can or should ignore the significance of the fact that a vast portion of our people believe in and worship God and that many of our legal, political, and personal values derive historically from religious teaching. Government must inevitably take cognizance of the existence of religion and indeed, under certain circumstances, the First Amendment may require that it do so." (Justice Goldberg)

"A strong case can certainly be made for the fact that there is injustice in taxing, for the support of public schools, those who send their children to private schools." (U. S. Senator Kenneth B. Keating)

"As a nation we must replace bitterness about the religious controversy in education with reason and careful thought; we must see to it that those who oppose each other talk with each other and talk constructively; we must seek out new approaches. Recognizing the basic decency of those between whom there is disagreement, all of us must—in a new spirit—join in seeking common ground." (Abraham Ribicoff)

"The right of the parent to attend to the child's education, is, moreover, antecedent to any human law or institution. It is vested in his very nature and is demanded as a fulfillment of his actual parenthood. . . . The private school is a concrete demonstration of the fact that education is not a monopoly of public authority." (American Catholic Bishops, 1955)

"Compromises must be made if a bill which meets the needs of the children of this great and varied nation is to be passed. But we must not compromise the Constitution. If we violate the separation of church and state and sacrifice an essential element in the maintenance of religious and civil liberty, we shall open a Pandora's box of domestic discord which may never be closed. Are the special interest groups prepared to sacrifice the welfare of the child to have their own way?" (*Christian Century*, 1961)

"If the pupil may fulfill his duty to the state by attending a parochial school, it is difficult to see why the state may not fulfill its duty to the pupil by encouraging it 'by all suitable means.' The state is under a duty to ignore the child's creed, but not its need. . . . The state which allows the pupil to subscribe to any religious creed should not, because of his exercise of this right, proscribe him from benefits common to all." (Mississippi State Court, 1941)

"I believe the wall of separation must be kept impregnable. The constitutional principle, and the need today as before, is for a complete and absolute separation. There is no place for compromise or 'degrees' of separation." (Kenneth W. Greenawalt, lawyer for ACLU)

"The public school system helped to forge a united nation. The parochial school system, if extended, shatters that unity, makes for separation and religious prejudices." (Sidney Hook)

"The American people will not permit this country's

long-standing traditions of Church and State separation to be scuttled. . . . [Aid to parochial schools] would demolish religious amity in this country, pitting church against church, brother against brother." (POAU, 1964)

"Every aristocratic, class-conscious private elementary school and every religious, parochial school is an enemy of the community and of our free institutions." (L. Harold DeWolf, Boston University School of Theology)

"Yet, there is no such thing—and there never was in American history—as a full, complete, definite, and thorough separation of church and state—decidedly not in educational matters. . . . [W]hen a principle, such as church-state separation has been consistently violated with common consent over the years, it is reasonable to inquire if it has not been downgraded to an *un-principle* or *anti-principle*." (William W. Brickman, New York University)

"The present accelerated program of parochial schools is not in the American tradition. It is an Old World import and does not fulfill the American dream of universal free education promoted by democratic principles and underwritten by all our citizens." (Maurice J. Thomas, University of Pittsburgh)

"It is high time, in the light of the cold reality of a long record of cooperation by the government and religion in educational affairs, to take a new look at the situation." (William W. Brickman)

"It is in homes and in schools that children are educated according to the principles of religion. After deciding that religion should be kept out of its schools, the State has now to deal with new generations who cannot educate because they themselves have lost the awareness of the religious foundations upon which their own education had been built. The bare fact is that, even where it survives, home education is no longer able to withstand alone the demoralizing pressure to which our children are now being submitted." (Etienne Gilson)

"The record of the past decade shows that the Sunday School does not adequately educate its pupils theologically or ecclesiastically. . . . The Protestant dependence for religious education on the Sunday School is proving that institution to be inadequate." (*Christian Century*)

"The only ground on which the Congress can legislate in this field is by reason of the general welfare and the security of all. Citizens of the several states are citizens of the United States and it is the policy of this nation to develop the capacity for educational excellence of every young American. This does not mean six out of seven or nine out of ten but every young American. The Congress is not bound and must not be bound by discriminatory state laws and outmoded customs in assisting every individual. The dollar must follow the child." (U.S. Representative Hugh L. Carey)

"No conceivable Congress would ever authorize financial aid to all private colleges *except* those having church affiliations. But I am not at all sure that the widely accepted distinction between aid to schools and aid to colleges can be justified in terms of constitutional principle." (Harry W. Jones, University of Chicago Law School)

"Enlightenment cannot occur when any important area of human life is excluded from serious, intelligent attention. However controversial, no area can rightly be excluded, whether it be politics, economics, morality or religion. . . . [T]he religious area of life is capable of enlightened study as well as any other. Thus the Lord's Prayer decision invites long overdue reconsideration of how public education may provide effective study of the role of religion in the experience of mankind. . . . It will need carefully trained teachers." (Theodore Brameld, Boston University)

"Our founding fathers never intended that our children be reared in a monolithic educational straightjacket. Our educational plant is a mosaic, with the free play of the many-faceted cultures of our people blending into the molding of an informed, dedicated, and loyal citizenry." (Rabbi Morris Sherer)

"In every large city certainly there should be an example or model of a Christian elementary school and a Christian high school, where the church shows the relationship of Christian truth to all human knowledge." (Conrad Bergendoff, Executive Secretary for Theological Education, Lutheran Church of America)

"Federal financial support of public education should follow the principle of restriction of public tax moneys to publicly controlled and supported schools." (American Association of School Administrators, 1963)

"The benefits of public welfare legislation may not be granted or denied to citizens because of their religious faith or lack of it." (Robert F. Drinan, S.J., Boston College Law School)

"Protestants and Roman Catholics alike have displayed a dog-in-the-manger attitude. Many Catholics oppose Federal aid to education unless they get their share, while Protestants tend to oppose experiments that might help to provide welfare services and secular education to parochial school children because they themselves are not organized to take advantage of such benefits. The whole debate is carried on in the context of a doctrinal discussion about church-state relations that does little to illuminate the basic issue." (John C. Bennett, Union Theological Seminary)

"I believe that simple justice requires that where the child goes, his share of the educational dollar should go. Since the state does not have the primary rights in the education of children, it follows the state does not have the sole claim on the educational tax dollar. I believe this principle is capable of translation into practice. I do not believe, as some opponents claim, it would decimate the public school system. I believe it would finally make the public school system better because it would require it to exist on funds set aside for the pupils it actually educates." (Dale Francis)

"The Amendment's purpose was to create a complete and permanent separation of the spheres of religious activity and civil authority." (Justice Rutledge, dissenting in *Everson*, 1947)

"The failure to discriminate between *distinguishing* and *separation* is one of the great obstacles to the advancement of real understanding." (Morris R. Cohen)

"To me it seems that the time has come to eliminate the bitterness that has developed in this fight on educational programs. If we don't eliminate this bitterness, we will never have an educational program in America." (Abraham Ribicoff)

"Giving Federal grants to private institutions of higher education is nothing new, and certainly not a radical departure from the previous national policy. To the contrary, giving grants to both public and private institutions has been the national policy for a century." (U.S. Representative Albert H. Quie)

"Compromises need to be worked out. There is room in our great democratic nation for both large-scale public and nonpublic systems." (Benjamin Fine, Brandeis University)

"There never existed any church-state-school separation in any meaningful sense of the term." (William W. Brickman)

"In no other program of government benefactions do we refer to recipients according to ethnic origins or credal profession. . . . Government is certainly not neutral when it taxes all to aid some and excludes others by a religious test." (Joseph F. Costanzo, S.J., Fordham University)

"The Constitution doesn't define limits, it says 'no establishment.' That means no state support for religious schools. . . . Tax exemption for religious institutions can in no wise be compared to funds for religious schools." (Rev. E. Paul Conine)

"To the believer—at least to many believers—the silent assumption by the public school that religion in any meaningful sense is irrelevant to the educational process amounts to an official establishment of secular values." (Robert Drinan)

"It is not beyond the wit of man, if he means it, for us to find a way of aiding education, whether it is in public schools or parochial schools, without getting involved in the question of teaching religion. We have to remember that we have laws in this country that every child must be educated, so we take that responsibility. We allow five million of them . . . to be educated in these parochial schools. They are part of the American system of education. . . . They should be educated as well as possible." (Walter Lippmann)

"I am one of those Jews who hopes with *America* that Jewish leaders will more constructively contribute to the solution of our dilemma; that religion may be more effectively related to public education, and more constructively influence our social order, without denial of freedom or infringement of conscience." (Rabbi Albert Gilbert)

"Institutions of public education disclose a considerable amount of religious influence at all levels. No matter what the constitutional theory, a good deal of religious doctrine finds its way into public school curricula." (F. Ernest Johnson)

"Dr. Conant is quoted as referring to the 'American principle of a single school system for all children.' I, an American of too many generations to count, never heard of that 'American principle.' We have certainly stood for education for all, regardless of social or economic status, but I should say that we have stood for liberty and individual freedom rather than the coercion implicit in a 'single public school system for all.'" (Nina Howell Starr)

"There is the opinion, and the authors share it, that if the Congress were to pass school aid legislation which provided assistance, directly or indirectly, to church-related schools, no one could ever successfully challenge the constitutionality of such a statute." (Paul M. Butler and Alfred L. Scanlan)

"It seems unfortunately to be the case that what has been presented as a means for preserving religious peace and freedom through secularization has to some extent become a method for propagating a particular dogmatic faith, namely, scientific naturalism or, to give it another name, naturalistic humanism." (Philip H. Phenix, Columbia University)

"Congress may withhold all sorts of facilities for a better life, but if it affords them it cannot make them available in an obviously arbitrary way or exact surrender of freedoms unrelated to the purpose of the facilities." (Justice Frankfurter)

"Whether a boy or girl gets a good education is just as important regardless of whether that boy or girl is a Catholic, Lutheran or Jewish. . . . Let's face up to it." (U.S. Senator Joseph S. Clark)

"We have . . . rejected the position of an absolute separation of church and state in favor of a mutually beneficial relationship in which each institution contributes to the general welfare and the common good by remaining true to its own nature and task." (Special Commission of the Lutheran Church in America, 1964)

"Children, regardless of religion, are still children and it seems only fair for government to be as interested in one group as in any other." (*Daily Standard*, Celina, Ohio)

"Some efforts making by disappointed orthodoxy to disaffect the public with the Board. They want, at least some of them, their own doctrines introduced. This cannot be, either theirs or those of any others, considered as sects merely." (Horace Mann)

". . . as the years passed, however, the conviction that sectarian indoctrination must be eliminated from the public school grew and triumphed; the educational and church leaders, as well as many statesmen, groped for a way to keep religion in and sectarianism out." (Msgr. William Kailer Dunn)

"Surely no human person would maintain that a hungry child should not receive a hot midday meal because he attends a Catholic school. And nobody should countenance, as has happened, that a bus driver should pick up some youngsters and be obliged to leave parochial school pupils stranded." (Agnes E. Meyer)

"When the First Amendment was passed, no public school system existed." (Anon.)

"Since I favor more strenuous competition between public and private schools, and more freedom of choice for parents, I should be inclined not to subsidize private any less than public schools." (Ernest van den Haag)

" . . . in view of constitutional and other restrictions, it would be in the best interests of public education to seek viable ways of securing better community cooperation between public and private institutions." (George N. Shuster)

"In any event, any categorical assertion that any fundamental assistance to parochial schools is unconstitutional cannot be supported by reference to any compelling authority. . . . Obviously, Congress cannot aid all education in promoting the general welfare if it leaves out of consideration the 6,752,000 children in nonpublic schools." (Paul G. Kauper, Michigan University Law School)

"We are a religious people whose institutions presuppose a supreme being. When the state encourages religious instruction or cooperates with religious authorities by adjusting the schedule of public events to sectarian needs, it follows the best of our traditions. To hold that it may not would be to find in the Constitution a requirement that the government show a callous indifference to religious groups. That would be preferring those who believe in no religion over those who do believe." (Justice Douglas, in *Zorach*, 1952)

"Our sects can live together in peace, not by ignoring each other as 'private,' but by recognizing and honoring one another as fellows in a common cause. Just as the teaching of geography is 'public,' so is the teaching of religion or nonreligion. In whatever varied ways are available, the general welfare requires that our young people learn the lessons which we call 'spiritual'. . . . [S]o long as half our people, more or less, are interpreting their lives, their family relationships, the upbringing of their children upon a basis of some religious belief, the Constitution requires of us that those beliefs shall be given not only equal status but also positive status in the public planning of education." (Alexander Meiklejohn, Wisconsin University)

"The Amendment . . . outlaws all use of funds for religious purposes." (Justice Rutledge, dissenting in *Everson*)

"It is not a question of religion, or of creed, or of party; it is a question of declaring and maintaining the great American principle of eternal separation of Church and State." (Elihu Root, 1894)

"Separation means separation, not something less." (Justice Black, in *McCollum*, 1948)

"The fact is that, for good or for ill, nearly everything in our culture worth transmitting, everything which gives meaning to life, is saturated with religious influences. . . . One can hardly respect a system of education that would leave the student wholly ignorant of the currents of religious thought that move the world society for a part in which he is being prepared." (Justice Jackson, concurring in *McCollum*)

"Thus, the 'wall of separation between church and state' that Mr. Jefferson built at the University which he founded did not exclude religious education from the school. The difference between the generality of his statements on the separation of church and state and the specificity of his conclusions on education are considerable. A rule of law should not be drawn from a figure of speech." (Justice Reed, dissenting in *McCollum*)

"It is not, however, to be understood that instruction

in religious opinion and duties was meant to be precluded by the public authorities, as indifferent to the interests of society. On the contrary . . . [the plan for the University] will give to the sectarian schools of divinity the full benefit of the public provisions . . . to establish their religious schools on the confines of the University . . . enabling the students of the University to attend religious exercises of their particular sect, either in the rooms of the building still to be erected . . . or in the lecturing room of each professor. . . . Such an arrangement would complete the circle of the useful sciences embraced by this institution, and would fill the chasm now existing, on principles which would leave inviolate the constitutional freedom of religion, the most inalienable and sacred of all human rights." (Thomas Jefferson)

"[The State] cannot exclude individual Catholics, Lutherans, Mohammedans, Baptists, Jews, Methodists, Non-believers, Presbyterians, or the members of any other faith, *because of their faith, or lack of it,* from receiving the benefits of public welfare legislation." (Justice Black, in *Everson*)

"Given the present world situation, this continuing mutual suspicion—even in its, thank God, attenuated form— constitutes a luxury that neither Jew nor Christian can afford." (Rabbi Marc H. Tanenbaum)

"The current controversy is a political argument in which, it seems to me, there are three substantial issues and one constitutional difficulty. The three substantial issues are the general welfare of the nation, the practical freedom of parental choice in education, and the equitable distribution of tax benefits to all school children without discrimination. The constitutional difficulty is created by the highly controverted interpretation of the establishment of religion clause of the First Amendment to the Constitution, announced for the first time in 1947 by the Supreme Court." (William J. Kenealy, S.J., Loyola University)

Readings

Much of the good recent literature on Church, State and school has been inspired by the *Everson* and the *McCollum* decisions, and has been written by legal experts for the legal journals. Following the prayer decisions, we may reasonably expect more of this challenging material. With article after article coming from legal and constitutional experts, it is a pity that, as a rule, even the educated public —teachers, journalists, clergymen, legislators—knows little, and that imperfectly and confusedly, about the history and status of the question.

We select some of the most useful and challenging books, mostly recent, on Church and State and school, on religion in public schools, and on what is being done in foreign countries. Our other selections are articles, many of them from professionals on law and the Constitution, among whom we signalize Ball, Butler and Scanlan, Corwin, Costanzo, Cushman, Katz, Kauper, Kenealy, Kurland, and Sutherland. The best articles on legal ethics and pluralism are those by Henle and Meiklejohn; the best on *Meyer* and *Pierce* is that by Bruère.

I. Books

Bailey, Stephen Kemp, and others. *School and Politics.* A study of state aid to education in the Northeast. Syracuse University Press, 1962.

Blanshard, Paul. *Religion and the Schools.* Boston: Beacon, 1963.

Blum, Virgil C. *Freedom of Choice in Education.* New York: Macmillan, 1958.

Brickman, William W. and Lehrer, Stanley (eds.). *Religion, Government, and Education.* New York: Society for the Advancement of Education, 1961.

Butts, R. Freeman. *The American Tradition in Religion and Education.* Boston: Beacon, 1950.

Dierenfield, Richard B. *Religion in American Public Schools.* Washington: Public Affairs Press, 1962.

Drinan, Robert F. *Religion, the Courts and Public Policy.* New York: McGraw, 1963.

Dubay, Thomas. *Philosophy of the State as Educator.* Milwaukee: Bruce, 1959.

Dunn, William Kailer. *What Happened to Religious Education?* Baltimore: Johns Hopkins Press, 1958.

Gabel, Richard J. *Public Funds for Church and Private Schools.* Washington: Catholic University, 1937; Toledo, Ohio: Murray and Heister, 1941.

Hansen, Carl Francis. *The Amidon School.* New York: Prentice-Hall, 1962.

Healey, Robert M. *Jefferson on Religion in Public Education.* Yale University Press, 1962.

Helmreich, Ernest C. *Religious Education in German Schools.* Harvard University Press, 1959.

Howe, Mark DeWolfe (ed.). *Cases on Church and State.* Harvard University Press, 1952.

Johnson, Alvin W. and Yost, Frank H. *Separation of Church and State in the United States.* University of Minnesota Press, 1934, 1946.

Johnson, Frederick Ernest (ed.). *American Education and Religion.* New York: Harper, 1952.

————— (ed.). *The Function of the Public Schools in Deal-*

ing with Religion. Washington: American Council on Education, 1953.

Kallen, Horace. *Cultural Pluralism and the American Idea.* University of Pennsylvania Press, 1956.

Katz, Wilber G. *Religion and American Constitutions.* Northwestern University Press, 1964.

Kauper, Paul. *Civil Liberties and the Constitution.* University of Michigan Press, 1962.

Littell, Franklin Hamlin. *From State Church to Pluralism.* Garden City: Doubleday, 1962.

McCluskey, Neil C. *Catholic Viewpoint on Education.* Garden City: Hanover, 1959.

Manwaring, David Roger. *Render unto Caesar.* The Flag-Salute Controversy. University of Chicago Press, 1962.

Murray, John Courtney. *We Hold These Truths.* New York: Sheed and Ward, 1960.

Oaks, D. H. (ed.). *The Wall between Church and State.* University of Chicago Press, 1963.

Pfeffer, Leo. *Church, State, and Freedom.* Boston: Beacon, 1953.

————. *Creeds in Competition.* New York: Harper, 1958.

Powell, Theodore. *The School Bus Case.* Wesleyan University Press, 1960.

Quattlebaum, Charles. *Federal Aid to Elementary and Secondary Education.* Washington: Public Affairs Bulletin, no. 61, 1948.

————. *Federal Scholarships and Fellowship Programs and other Government Aids to Students.* Washington: United States Printing Office, 1950.

Religion in the Schools. New York: Fund for the Republic, 1959.

Ryan, Mary Perkins. *Are Parochial Schools the Answer?* New York: Holt Rinehart, 1963.

Sacks, Benjamin. *The Religious Issue in the State Schools of England and Wales, 1902–1914.* A Nation's Quest for Human Dignity. University of New Mexico Press, 1961.

Tussman, Joseph. *The Supreme Court on Church and State* (readings). Oxford University Press, 1962.

Ward, Leo R. *Religion in All the Schools.* Notre Dame, Ind.: Fides, 1960.

II. Articles

Axtelle, George. "Religion, Education, and Culture." *Educational Forum,* 21 (Nov. 1956), 5–17.

Ball, William B., and others. "The Constitutionality of the Inclusion of Church-Related Schools in Federal Aid to Education." *Georgetown Law Review,* 50 (Winter, 1961), 401–455. Also available at National Catholic Welfare Conference, 1312 Massachusetts Ave. N.W., Washington, D. C.

Blum, Virgil C. "Religious Liberty and the Religious Garb." *University of Chicago Law Review,* 22 (Summer, 1955), 875–895.

Boyer, William W. "Sectarian Teachers in Wisconsin Public Schools." *Religious Education,* 57 (May-June, 1962), 195–202.

Brickman, William W. "The School and the Church-State Question." *School and Society,* 71 (May 6, 1950), 273–292.

Bruère, Robert W. "The Supreme Court on Educational Freedom." *Survey,* 54 (July 1, 1925), 379–381.

Butler, Paul M. and Scanlan, Alfred L. "Wall of Separation—Judicial Gloss on the First Amendment." *Notre Dame Lawyer,* 37 (March, 1962), 288–308.

Corwin, Edward S. "The Supreme Court as National School Board." *Thought,* 43 (Dec. 1948), 665–683. Slightly revised in *Law and Contemporary Problems,* 14 (1949), 3–22.

Costanzo, Joseph. "Federal Aid to Education and Religious Liberty." *University of Detroit Law Review,* 36 (Oct. 1959), 3–46.

————. "Religion in Public Education." *Thought,* 31 (Summer, 1956), 216–244.

————. "Ribicoff on Federal Aid to Education." *Thought,* 356 (Winter, 1961), 485–536.

————. "Thomas Jefferson, Religious Education and Public Law." *Journal of Public Law,* 8 (Spring, 1959), 81–108.

Creegan, Robert F. "Subsidized Pluralism." *School and Society*, 86 (Jan. 18, 1958), 34–36.

Crotty, Homer D. "The Tuition Tax Credit Plan: Sound Aid for the College and Law Schools." *American Bar Association Journal* (Nov. 1961).

Cushman, Robert Fairfield. "Public Support of Religious Education in American Constitutional Law." *Illinois Law Review*, 45 (1950–51), 333–356.

Degler, Carl N. "Why Not Federal Aid to Parochial Schools?" *Vassar Alumnae Magazine*, 47 (Feb. 1963), 2–7.

Donahue, Charles. "Freedom and Education: The Pluralistic Background." *Thought*, 27 (1952), 542–560.

Drinkwater, F. H. "School Aid in England." *Commonweal*, 75 (Oct. 6, 1961), 38–42.

"Federal Aid for All the Schools." American Press, 1962.

Freedom in Education (formerly *Fair Share News*). Published by Citizens for Educational Freedom, 3109 Grand Blvd., St. Louis 18, Mo.

Friedman, Milton. "Role of Government in Education." A chapter in *Economics and the Public Interest*. Ed. by Robert Solo. Rutgers University Press, 1955.

Griswold, Erwin N. "On Church and State." *America*, 108 (March 1963), 374–375.

Hayes, John C. "The Constitutional Permissibility of the Participation of Church-Related Schools in the Administration's Proposed Program of Federal Aid to Education." *De Paul Law Review*, 11 (Spring-Summer, 1962), 161–182.

Henle, R. J. "American Principles and State Neutrality." *St. Louis University Law Journal*, 3 (Spring, 1955), 237–251.

Hutchins, "The Future of the Wall." *America*, 108 (Jan. 26, 1963), 146–148.

Johnson, F. Ernest. "Policies and Recommendations of the American Council on Education Committee on Religion and Education." *Religious Education*, 57 (July-Aug. 1957), 247–255.

Katz, Wilber G. "Freedom of Religion and State Neutrality." *University of Chicago Law Review*, 20 (Spring, 1953), 426–440.

————. "The Freedom to Believe." *Atlantic Monthly*, 192 (Oct. 1953), 66–69.

Kauper, Paul G. "Church and State Cooperative Separatism." *Michigan Law Review*, 60 (Nov. 1961), 1–40.

————. "The Constitutionality of Aid to Parochial Schools." *Phi Delta Kappan*, 43 (May, 1962), 331–336.

Kenealy, William J. "Equal Justice under Law." *The Catholic Lawyer*, 7 (Summer, 1961), 183–202.

Kohlbrenner, Bernard J. "The Controversy over Public Support to Parochial Schools." *School and Society*, 89 (May 20, 1961), 238–242.

Kurland, Philip B. "Of Church and State and the Supreme Court." *University of Chicago Law Review*, 29 (Autumn, 1961), 1–96. With corrections and additions, published as a book, *Religion and the Law*. Chicago: Aldine Pub. Co., 1962.

"Meaning of Religion in the First Amendment," *Catholic World*, 197 (Aug. 1963), 276–317.

Meiklejohn, Alexander. "Educational Cooperation between Church and State." *Law and Contemporary Problems*, 14 (1949), 61–72.

Murray, John Courtney. "The Catholic University in a Pluralist Society." *Catholic Mind*, 57 (June, 1959), 253–260.

————. "Making of a Pluralistic Society." *Religious Education*, 53 (1958), 521–528.

————. "The State University in a Pluralistic Society." *Catholic Mind*, 57 (June, 1959), 242–252.

Paulsen, Monrad G. "Preferment of Religious Institutions in Tax and Labor Legislation." *Law and Contemporary Problems*, 14 (1949), 144–159.

"Public Funds for Parochial Schools?" National Council of Churches. 1963.

Rheinberger, Henry P. "Parents' Right to Educate the Child." *Oklahoma Law Review*, 13 (Nov. 1960), 432–434.

Rice, Arthur. "Are Shared Facilities the Answer?" *The Nation's Schools*, 69 (June, 1962).

Rossi, Peter H. and Alice S. "Some Effects of Parochial School Education in America." *Daedalus*, 90 (Spring, 1961), 300–329.

Stearns, Harry L. "Shared Time: A Proposal for the Education of Children." *Religious Education*, 57 (Jan.-Feb., 1962), 5–10.

Stopford, Robert W., Yeaxlee, Basil, Drinkwater, F. H., and others. "Religious Education in England." *Religious Education*, 56 (March-April, 1961), 114–143.

Sutherland, Arthur E., Jr. "Due Process and Disestablishment." *Harvard Law Review*, 62 (June, 1949), 1306–1344.

Ulich, Robert, Kandel, I. L., and others. "Government and Education Abroad." *Current History*, 40 (June, 1961), 321–360.

Index

A NOTE ON THE TYPE

IN WHICH THIS BOOK IS SET

This book is set in Janson, a Linotype face, created from the early punches of Anton Janson, who settled in Leipzig around 1670 This type is not an historic revival, but rather a letter of fine ancestry, remodelled and brought up to date to satisfy present day taste. It carries a feeling of being quite compact and sturdy. It has good color and displays a pleasing proportion of ascenders and descenders as compared to the height of the lower case letters. The book was composed and printed by The York Composition Company, Inc., of York, Pa., and bound by Moore and Company of Baltimore. The typography and design are by Howard N. King.